LADIES

FIRST

LADIES FIRST

REVELATIONS OF A STRONG WOMAN

QUEEN LATIFAH

WITH KAREN HUNTER

Foreword by Rita Owens

WILLIAM MORROW AND COMPANY, INC.

NEW YORK

Library of Congress Cataloging-in-Publication Data

Latifah, Queen.
    Ladies first : revelations of a strong woman / by Queen Latifah with Karen Hunter : foreword by Rita Owens.
        p.   cm.
    ISBN 0-688-15623-1
    1. Self-esteem in women.   2. Latifah, Queen.   I. Hunter, Karen.
II. Title.
    HQ1206.L375 1999
    158.1'082—dc21   98-41533
                                                                  CIP

Printed in the United States of America

First Edition

1   2   3   4   5   6   7   8   9   10

BOOK DESIGN BY CAROLINE CUNNINGHAM

www.williammorrow.com

To every woman who has ever felt like less than royalty

CONTENTS

■ ■ ■

ACKNOWLEDGMENTS

■ ■ ■

Praise and thanks go first to God, the original Queen and Creator of all.

Praise and thanks go to my mother, Rita Owens, the best example any girl could have; to my father, Lancelot Owens, who gave me the strength to explore this world from another perspective; and to my brother, Winki, who paved the way for me and continues to be my inspiration.

I'd like to thank Karen Hunter for coming in at the last minute and pulling all this together. You are a creative genius, girl. Thanks to Doris Cooper for having the vision for this book and the tenacious spirit to make it happen. Thanks to my right hand, arm, and leg, Shakim Compere. And thanks to my lawyer, Stewart Levy, and my agent, Denise Stinson.

Thanks to Ramsey and Tammy and Julie, my buddies for life. To L.B. for making the schedules work out, for running interference through the most difficult situations, and for being my friend.

Finally, thanks to the entire Flavor Unit: DJ Mark the 45 King, Lisa, Apache, Latee, Paul, Chill Rob G, Double J, the whole Naughty Crew, and Kaygee—y'all taught me how and encouraged me throughout.

Peace.

FOREWORD
by Rita Bray Owens

■ ■ ■

From the very beginning, I knew my daughter was going to be different. Dana refused to be born. She was due around February 25 but didn't come until March 18— under threat of induced labor. Ten long months I carried her. I finally had to tell the doctors to go in and get her. And she fought that, too. She was eight pounds, three ounces, with a mind of her own from day one.

And I loved her.

I bought a baby book to record everything from her first steps to her first words. I treasured her early pictures, her baby footprints, and the soft silky hair that covered her infant head. In my mind, she was from God. I thought of her as my little miracle.

When she was a little less than a year old, I sat down and wrote a two-page letter to Dana. I wanted her to look back some day and to know just how joyous I felt to have her in my life.

"She is the most amazing little child I have ever seen,"

I wrote. "She's even more active than Winki. I can't believe I could be so blessed, not once, but twice."

As I look back, I realize that subconsciously I was building Dana's self-esteem from the day she was born. She and my son were the most precious parts of my life, and I wanted to set them up to win.

When Dana became an active child, she always wanted to explore the parts of the world that don't normally interest little girls. She was the little sheep who is always wandering away from the flock.

Her first foray was into the martial arts. She was dying to take karate lessons—just like her brother. I was afraid she would get hurt. All those rough boys kicking and punching in a big room didn't seem like the place for my Dana. But I never stopped her. I kept my fears to myself and encouraged her. I was mindful not to interfere with her desires—no matter how unconventional they may have been.

The next foray was a little more traditional. When she was in third grade, Dana came home and said she wanted ballet lessons and to learn how to play the guitar. At least she wouldn't be getting beat up, but now I had to worry about how to afford the lessons.

I did not say no. I wanted my daughter to hear "yes," not excuses about why she could not have something—or worse, why she could not *do* something. So I found a community center that provided dance and music lessons where the fee was based on the family's income.

Unlike most teenagers, who want to blend in with their peers, Dana followed her own beat. When her brother went out to play baseball and basketball, he took his sister. The other kids called her a tomboy, but I never let her accept that moniker. I didn't want to see my little girl's feelings get hurt, and a big part of me wanted to protect her—to tell her to come inside where she wouldn't be ridiculed. But you can't hide your kids from the world or shield them because of your own experiences. I told her to tell them, "I'm not a tomboy—I'm just an athlete." I wanted her to stick up for herself. I would not allow Dana to buy into any negativity or let someone else make her into something she wasn't.

The best way I could protect her was by showing her how to stick up for herself. I knew that she was going to run into a lot of battles in her years—because that's life—and I wanted her to see right from the start that she could take them on.

Just as I did not want her to let others label her, I did not want her to be afraid to define herself.

I learned early on just what Dana wasn't. When she was little, I would dress her in prissy outfits, complete with bows in her hair and matching bobby socks. By the end of the day, the bows would be either missing or knocked to the side and the socks rolled down and dirty. She'd have chocolate around her mouth and spots on her dress. I knew then there was no use forcing my daughter to be dainty. She was who she was.

I got a dynamo.

Dana's daintiness was internal. She had softness and gentleness. They were very much a part of my daughter's character. If you told Dana she had disappointed you, she would shed tears. She was, above all, sensitive.

Even at age seven she was compassionate and kind.

One time, Dana brought home a cocker spaniel she had found while out playing. The dog didn't have a collar or a license. It was just a pedigreed stray—mangy and hyper—and I really did not want it in my house. But Dana insisted on keeping it. She felt a kinship with this poor dog, whose mouth was dripping with honey (now, where'd this dog get honey?) when I first saw it.

I let her keep it.

Dana named the dog Silky. This dog was mental. He would jump into our car and wouldn't let us get in. He'd bark and growl as if we were from animal control. When my parents came to visit us from Virginia, the dog somehow jumped into their car, and it took us an hour and a half to get him out. We were laughing, but my parents didn't see the humor. They felt I was being a pushover, letting Dana keep a psychotic dog. They were right and wrong. I *was* being a pushover—it would have been much easier to lay down the law with my girl and just say no, the dog has to go. But I didn't want to take away from her something that she loved and was responsible for. I wanted her to know what it was like to care for something and have it depend on her. I wanted Dana to know a mutual need.

Silky the psychopath finally ran away. I cried superficial tears for Dana's sake. I was so happy, I wanted to light a bonfire. But Dana was crushed.

So what some couldn't understand, but that I, as her mother, knew, was that my daughter was strong on the outside, but soft as a down pillow on the inside.

Yet within that gentle girl was also a fierce independence. I first saw it when Dana was in kindergarten. The school she attended was great, but the neighborhood was questionable. As the kids left the school yard and filed back into the classroom building, the teachers would lock the door to the school behind the last student. Of course Dana, being the tallest in her class, was the last in line. One day she became distracted and separated from the line of kids. Before she knew it, she was locked out of the school.

I was at work, and unbeknownst to me my poor baby was out there all alone. Not knowing where else to go, she headed for the closest safe haven—"Grandma's house." Unfortunately, this was a one and a half mile trek. She walked from High Street in Newark across Broad Street, a major four-lane drag; down a long hill; and all the way to her grandmother's house. A couple of people helped her cross the streets, but no one thought to find out what this little person was doing out in the middle of the business district by herself in the middle of the day.

It wasn't the best route for walking, but it was the only way she knew. She was five years old, and somehow she remembered the car route. She got to the house—tired and frightened. All her grandmother and aunt heard was this little voice crying through the mail slot, "Grandma! Grandma!" They called me at work, and I rushed to the house. I was frantic and scared. But when I saw her little face and smothered her with a million hugs and kisses, all I could say to her was what I was feeling: "You are a remarkable little girl. You are something else!" I knew then that Dana could think for herself and deal with unforeseen situations as they arose.

I, like many women, grew up not knowing who I was. I was never sure of myself. I was the middle child of seven—five brothers and an older sister—and I was lost in a household of men and strong women. My mother was a housekeeper, and my father was an army sergeant. They were strict disciplinarians who worked very hard. I always felt loved and encouraged, but just another one of Sergeant Bray's childern.

I was the classic, weird middle child. When everybody else wanted peanut butter and jelly, I'd want jelly and jelly.

Lunch requests: baloney and mustard, baloney and mustard, baloney and mustard; then they'd get to me: dry bread. My family simply accepted me for me and tended to overlook rather than investigate the times I marched to the beat of a different drummer.

With seven kids, it was enough to work and feed and clothe us all, let alone figure out why we were the way we were. We were defined by each other; no one encouraged me to be my own person. If the oldest three got A's in math, then it was my responsibility to get an A in math, too. It didn't matter that I wanted to be an artist and couldn't care less about math.

I didn't know who Rita was as an individual. I was always somebody's younger sister, somebody's older sister, somebody's daughter. I knew I liked art and wanted to be a teacher, but I didn't know where Rita fit in the grand scheme of things. And I didn't have the verbal skills to express those concerns to my parents so that they could better help me maximize my potential.

My parents were from the old school where children did as they were told and were not involved in grown folks' business unless my father had called a family meeting. You kept your opinion to yourself, and if you were going to roll your eyes, you better not get caught doing it. We did sit around the dinner table talking about life and the world we could not see but that was there for us to discover, but there were definitely no discussions about sex. The fast girls, the ones who managed to get the well-worn love magizines that had been passed through many hands, were my occasional source of knowledge. The magazines were fiction and the girls knew even less about practical human sexuality.

I was curious about my son, and I was curious about Dana. Their actions fascinated me, and I needed to know what motivated them. I studied them because I wanted to know just how to prepare them to make decisions about their future. Like any parent, I wanted my children to go to school, get a job, and live happily ever after. But in the quest to make them active, productive members of society, I did not want to lose sight of the heart. That's where happiness is going to come from. Above all, I wanted my children to love what they saw in the mirror.

But how does a parent do that? Surely it is more easily said than done. I started by giving my son and daughter a healthy amount of freedom and encouraging them to question me so that we could have a dialogue—the dialogue that was often absent in my household when I was a child.

I wanted Dana to feel that there was nothing she couldn't talk to me about. And there wasn't. She told me about her first kiss. She came tiptoeing into the kitchen, real secretive. "Ma," she whispered, "guess what? I have something to tell you."

"What, baby?" I asked.

"I got a kiss," she said.

She was eleven years old. Now, a million questions raced through my head. Being the nosy mother, I needed to know what was involved in that kiss—was it a French kiss, was there any groping? I wanted to keep the door open for dialogue and not risk putting her on the defensive, so I kept quiet and let her do the talking. I got real excited for her and said, "Oh yeah? What did he say? How did it happen?" At that point, we were friends, instead of mother and daughter. You don't tell your mother the good stuff.

I found out that the kiss was really only a peck. Innocent. The boy ran home after he had planted one on her cheek. It was cute. And I felt good that she had confided in me. That conversation with Dana was a very intimate moment. It was an indicator of our relationship. It allowed me to figure out what I needed to do—whether I should move the conversation to the next level, whether we were ready to have "that talk."

I wanted my door always to be open to her.

In order to do that, I had to swallow a lot, too. I would say to Dana, "If you tell me the truth, you won't get in trouble." And she would tell me the truth. The truth sometimes hurt and even shocked me, but I had to keep my word. Not long after Dana transferred to Irvington High School, where I taught, I found out she had cut class and taken a trip with some buddies into New York. When I confronted her, she confessed. I wanted to slam-dunk her butt on the spot. But I didn't. Instead I looked at the components: We have a great relationship. I work at the school.

She must have known I would catch her. None of this made any sense. It was more important for me to find out the "why" than to punish her and have her do it again and again.

We talked but I got on this "me" thing—"You're doing this to humiliate me!" But what I found out by discussing her actions was that they weren't personal. They weren't about me. She had a thirst for street knowledge that was bigger than even me. Her cutting class and running to New York was her way of spreading her wings. But that didn't make me like it one bit. She had jeopardized the trust of our relationship and put herself in the danger that comes with being fourteen years old, looking like an adult, and running the streets of Manhattan thinking you know everything. It was a lot. But I had to pray, give her over to God, and know that she was His child and He would take care of her.

This was not easy. But there's a point where a parent simply can do no more than pray. After the talking, the arguing, the threatening, the punishing, there's really nothing left to do with an independent child. I had to trust that higher being. I had to trust my child. I had to trust that I had raised her with a solid moral and spiritual foundation that would eventually set her on the right path.

Honesty builds trust, and that in turn builds self-esteem and confidence. I'm not happy about everything Dana did, and I am not pleased with the end result of all of our conversations. But I couldn't bash her over the head with my opinion just because I didn't like what she was doing. Sometimes I just had to listen, no matter how I was feeling inside, because it was important that she express herself. I had to bury my motherly, judgmental side and be objective to really hear what she was saying so that I could help her. And trust me, this was no easy task.

The road to solid self-esteem and self-confidence starts with dialogue in the home, and it starts in the womb. It does not come from criticizing your child's actions constantly or from judging her every mistake. Constantly fighting and punishing were only going to alienate us from each other. And I wanted, more than anything, for us to be a part of each other's lives. How else would I be able to nourish her spiritually and emotionally?

Your child is like anything else; you get out what you put in.

In my classes at Irvington High School, I've had many students with low self-esteem, who felt worthless. They were usually the "shy" ones. I would single them out to help me with projects or make them the assistant to the substitute teacher. Also give them honest praise: "You accomplished so much work today—good job," or "Girl, those shoes are too cute," or "Thanks so much for your help. I couldn't have done it without you."

One student found out that I liked Sweetarts, which then cost just a nickel. Several times a week she would give me some and would never take any money. "You are so sweet," I would tell her. "You're too good to me." I didn't give her an A or any other special treatment. She didn't think she would get anything out of it; she was simply being nice. And I wanted to encourage that in her. I could see her eyes brighten and watch her stand a little taller every time my positive words came her way.

Encouraging comments can do wonders for a person's self-esteem. You get him to recognize the positive things about himself that he may not have even noticed.

The older you get, the less often you're going to get that pat on the back. So you have to learn at a young age to give it to yourself. I want to make sure that the people around me, particularly my own kids and the students I teach, get that pat on the back and learn to give it to others and to themselves. That's how the cycle begins—you praise them, and they will be kind and gentle to others. You're never too old for praise.

Every year in my class, I do an exercise in which I make each student write down ten things that he or she thinks are positive about him or herself. It's amazing how many kids have never given any thought to their inner qualities. I even start them off with a few things I see in them individually. And there are a few things that I give to everyone:

1. God don't make no junk; it's that simple.
2. I was born for greatness.

3. I am beautiful in my own right.
4. I am unique; there is no one else exactly like me.
5. I can do and be anything I want.

Of course, this is high school. But adults need to embrace this philosophy, too. Sit down once in a while and examine what makes you beautiful, no matter what your age. There is a time in everyone's life when one needs to evaluate and reevaluate oneself. You don't want to start off by beating yourself up because you haven't accomplished everything you thought you should have. It's best to start by accentuating the positive; that will help with the reevaluation process. Writing down your attributes is a way to see exactly what you have accomplished. Then you can look at where you've been and where you are and begin to figure out where you're going—and set new goals. That's why knowing yourself is so important.

I wasn't exactly thrilled when my daughter told me she was quitting college for a little while to become a rapper. A rapper? Queen *what*? But I had to give her the freedom to pursue her goal, because I knew she was a remarkable, confident young woman. She was determined, and I wasn't going to take that away from her.

Dana went to the Borough of Manhattan Community College for a year and a half. She was studying communications. But the opportunities in the music industry—

travel and the chance to experience a world that she otherwise might not—represented an offer that we couldn't refuse. To me, that was life education. But it was also extremely daunting. It meant serious business meetings with strangers and being judged on everything from talent to looks to image by an industry that was notoriously unforgiving.

Dana had the confidence to face the unknown and to get in there and be herself without selling out, because she always had strong women around her. She knew her great-grandmother, who was a live-in servant and a proud woman who didn't take any shorts. She saw it in my mother (Nana) and in her father's mother. She saw it in the cleaning lady at Kean College, who used to take Dana and Winki on her rounds so that I could concentrate on earning my degree in Art Education.

She knew Dr. Elaine Raichle, the woman who gave me my first opportunity to teach. Dr. Raichle saw more in me than I saw in myself. She was a woman of character whose mere presence influenced my daughter. So did Mary Jane Austin, my mentor and also an art education administrator, as well as Rose Schell, who allowed her to teach Spanish to her peers at Irvington High School. These women, among the many aunts and godmothers, represent the "village that raised my child." Because of their vision, these women, whom you do not read about in the history books, provided components for success that I alone could not. These mediators of tough love and nurturing served as community success stories for future reference when Dana began to claim her place in a male-dominated arena.

Dana knew all these strong women. But she also learned from the weak. She has seen what happens when good people make bad decisions or throw their lives away. She has a cousin who is addicted to heroin. Dana loves her with all her heart and is terribly upset when she sees her on drugs. She is a wonderful person. But I told Dana, "Sometimes it's about choices. It's not always about how good or bad you are, but about the choices you make."

I believe everyone starts out with an inner confidence, and then life—parents, friends, family, tragedy—chips away at it. This could start with lack of praise for a job well done. Or false accusations. It doesn't have to be a major thing to mess you up. When I went to visit Dana's elderly grandmother in the hospital, she told me about something that had happened to her when she was a child. Her older cousin lied and said she had broken her father's watch. Her father believed her cousin, and he slapped his daughter in the face. He had never hit her before, and she was devastated that her father would take the word of her cousin over her own. Dana's grandmother withdrew from those family members for the rest of her life, it hurt her so deeply. Almost eighty years have passed, and she has never forgotten it nor how it made her feel. That incident stunted her growth, alienated her from family members. There was a betrayal of trust. He didn't trust her to tell the truth and their relationship paid the price.

Every child has the right to feel confident, and as adults we must take on the responsibility to see that that happens. It doesn't have to be a loud, singing, performing confidence. It can also be a quiet "You can trust me to do the right thing when I'm with my peers" kind of confidence.

Many of my students ask me why I still teach. "You're Queen Latifah's mother; you don't have to work," they say. I tell them, "Rita does what God told her to do. And Latifah does what God told *her* to do."

My daughter, Dana Elaine Owens, took her life experiences and followed her dream because she had the freedom to explore and the confidence to fly.

Rita Bray Owens has been a teacher for more than eighteen years at Irvington High School, where she has taught art and life to thousands of young people. In 1986, Ms. O, as she is affectionately known, founded the Urban Youth Coalition, an organization with a mission to teach students about self-esteem, cultural diversity, conflict resolution, leadership skills, and academic excellence. Her efforts garnered her an Excellence in Teaching Award from New Jersey Governor

Christine Todd Whitman and a Role Model of the Year Award from Lincoln University.

Ms. O founded the Lancelot H. Owens Scholarship Foundation in memory of her only son, who died in a motorcycle accident in 1992. The foundation raises money to send hundreds of inner-city youth to college each year.

When she isn't teaching, Ms. O is vice president of Flavor Unit Entertainment, a company started by Queen Latifah and her former student Shakim Compere that manages such artists as LL Cool J, Outkast, and Next.

LADIES FIRST

■ ■ ■

INTRODUCTION

''Who You Callin'
a Bitch?''

I am not a psychologist or a sociologist. I don't have any degrees, and I'm not an expert on life. What I am is a young black woman from the inner city who is making it, despite the odds, despite the obstacles I've had to face in the lifetimes that have come my way.

I have lived in housing projects and in fine homes. I have hung out with drug dealers and with presidents. I have had to clean bathrooms for a living. And I've had my own maid. I've sold millions of records and have won a Grammy. I've made movies that have bombed. I've had to

1

bury my big brother, Winki. And I've also wanted to die myself. I've felt low, and I've felt on top of the world.

Through it all, though, I never forget who I am. The one thing that has kept me going is knowing who I am.

I am a child of God. I am a queen.

A queen is a queen when riding high, and when clouded in disgrace, shame, or sorrow, she has dignity. Being a queen has very little to do with exterior things. It is a state of mind. And with God as the center of your life, you can never be dethroned.

I'm writing this book to let every woman know that she, too—no matter what her status or her place in life—is royalty. This is particularly important for African-American women to know inside and out, upside down, and right side up. For so long in this society, we have been given—and have allowed ourselves to take—the role of slave, concubine, mammy, second-class citizen, bitch, ho. Many of us have been so hurt and so dogged out by society—and by men and by life—that we can't even wrap our brains around the notion that we deserve better, that we are queens.

All things start inside your soul and work outward. Thoughts are powerful. Words are powerful. As a rapper, I've learned that what you put out in the spoken and in the written word is what you'll get back. That's why I keep my music positive. I want to uplift, I want to inform.

> Instincts lead me to another flow
> Every time I hear a brother call a girl a bitch or a ho.
> Trying to make a sister feel low,
> You know all of that's got to go.
> Now everybody knows there's exceptions to this rule.
> Now don't be getting mad
> When we're playing, it's cool.
> But don't you be callin' me out my name
> I bring wrath to those who disrespect me like a dame.
> —"U.N.I.T.Y."

I won a Grammy, an NAACP Image Award, and a Soul Train Music Award in 1994 for this song. But I didn't write it to win awards. I wrote it because all around I saw women being verbally and physically assaulted, especially in rap music. Gangsta rap was ruling at the time, and with it came all this misogynistic bull—*bitch* this, *ho* that. And crazy as it sounds, I saw female rappers buying into it. There was even a group that called itself BWA—Bitches With Attitude. Other groups were disrespecting *them* in their raps, and these ladies didn't even defend themselves in their music. They took it. What kind of a message was that sending?

I had something to say to everybody in my music. But I decided to address the ladies first. We have the power to set the men straight. If you don't feel like a bitch, no one can call you that and make it stick. I realized it was more important to start building women up and making them look inside themselves than to bash the fellas. It starts with our own self-esteem, and too many women don't have any.

I learned at an early age that nobody has the right to call me out of my name. The first time some kid around my way called me a tomboy, I went home crying to my mother. She comforted me and then sent me on my way. She told me to go back out there. "Tell that boy you're *not* a tomboy; you're just athletic!" That didn't go over too well with the kids around my way, but it didn't matter. I made my point. I don't have to accept somebody else's moniker for me. I define who I am. My mom planted a seed in my head that day.

Sometimes all it takes is someone to tell you that you don't have to take it. Sometimes all it takes is a word to instill self-confidence and self-esteem in someone. For me, it was my parents telling me I could do anything. It was having a brother, two years older, who egged me on to dare to experience different things. He was adventurous and taught me that the more you try, the more surface area you create in which to succeed. And from success, you gain self-confidence.

I was scared the first time I went onstage, in a talent show at Irvington High School. I couldn't breathe, and I broke out into an instant sweat at the thought of going out in front of all those people. What if they don't like me? What if somebody boos? Those questions are usually enough to get people to hide behind the curtain and never come out onstage. Instead I turned it around. What if they love me? What if they give me a standing ovation? Both my lack of self-confidence and my abundance of it were speaking at the same time. The latter won out.

I loved singing, and I wanted to know if other people would enjoy the music I made as much as I did. I would never know if I really had talent unless I went out there. I took that stage and sang "If Only for One Night" by Luther Vandross. I focused on a smiling face in the crowd. I didn't know the person, but he was encouraging me, and I took it. I got that standing ovation. The next time I stood onstage, I was still scared, but not as much.

There's nothing wrong with being afraid. There *is* something wrong—definitely wrong—with being so afraid that you don't even try. I've always been more afraid of *not* trying something. If you try and fail, at least you know what you can't do, and it leaves you room to attempt something else and keep going for it until you find your niche. But if you never try, that's the biggest failure.

I once jumped off a fifty-foot cliff in Jamaica. I was on vacation in Negril in the summer of 1996—one of the few vacations I've had. I had lunch at Rick's Café, which overlooks the ocean. It is surrounded by cliffs, and people dive off them while others sit in the café, eating and watching.

I was a spectator at first. But crazy me decided to join those divers before I ate. I had on a bathing suit and some gym shorts. I walked over to the tiny platform and waited for a Rasta, who must have been a professional diver, to jump. He did a beautiful dive into the water that ended in barely a splash. He looked like a Rasta Greg Louganis. Then it was my turn. When I looked down, I had second thoughts. From up there, it felt like I was jumping off the Empire State Building. I was dizzy.

Behind me, toward the restaurant, I noticed a crowd forming. A couple of people recognized me. I saw Washington Wizards basketball star Juwann Howard and his crew pointing. They had a great view of me from their table.

Shakim Compere, my manager, business partner, and one of my oldest friends, was there with me. He looked over and said, "No freaking way!" He refused to jump. By this point, I was terrified. But I wanted to test the limits. It wasn't so much that I wanted to see if I could dive off the cliff—that took only a jump—but I needed to know if I could be brave enough to overcome my fear.

I jumped, feet first. About halfway down, I thought I ran out of breath. There was silence for what seemed like an hour. I felt like I was going in slow motion. I thought I would die. Then—SPLASH! I hit that water. And it was like somebody sucker punched my entire body. And I had a wedgie from hell.

When I came out of the water, I was exhilarated. Until I realized that I was trapped. The stairs leading back to the restaurant were on the other side of where I had landed, and the only way to get there was to swim across, climb up the rocks again, and dive from the other side. This time, I was ready to do it. There were a couple of people up there, and we all held hands and jumped together.

I had conquered the fear, which was what I had set out to do in the first place.

I'm afraid all the time. I'm afraid of being alone. I'm afraid of commitment. I'm afraid of failure. I'm afraid of becoming someone I'm not in the music business. I'm afraid of not having a child before I get too old. But none of these fears rules my life. Fear is a breeding ground for fear. If you don't control it, it will control you. One of the books that has influenced me the most is *Feel the Fear and Do It Anyway* by Dr. Susan Jeffers. She says we have the power to create anything and that there are aspects of our lives we cannot control. But we *can* control how we handle them. If I wake up and it's dark and gloomy outside, do I lie there and complain about how nasty the day is? Or do I say, "Hey, I'm going to go out and have a good time today"? We can control an enormous amount: our attitude, perspective, actions—and we must control them. It may seem like common sense, but think about how often we allow outside influences to dampen our attitude and mess with our perspective.

We've all done things we know we shouldn't have, simply because we chose not to think about them or because we ignored an inner voice—perhaps it was *easier* to be passive than to control our actions. I am not afraid to hear the truth and hold myself accountable to that truth. I am never afraid of pushing myself to be my best.

But how do fear, pride, and determination make Dana Owens a queen, you ask? And what right does *anyone* have to call herself a queen without sounding like one helluvan arrogant sista? Well, first of all, each of us has a queen inside. She was placed there before we were even formed, in the womb. It's just a matter of bringing her out. Being a woman puts you halfway there. But there's so much more. It starts inside by feeling good about yourself. A queen has high self-esteem. She is proud of who she is, whether she is a corporate executive or a cleaning lady, whether she's an athlete or a housewife.

She knows right from wrong and strives to do her best. She doesn't player-hate, or try to put other women down. Women have a tendency to be catty or jealous of what other women are doing or have. They will sleep with another woman's man "just because." They will have a nasty attitude toward another woman and say things like "She thinks she's cute!" Well, that ain't cute. A real queen is so focused on keeping herself tight that she doesn't have time to be worried about the next one. A real queen is so intent on raising herself up that she can be proud of what her sisters are doing, because she's okay with herself and with God.

Queenliness is an attitude that starts on the inside and works its way out. The way you hold your head up makes you a queen. It says something about how you feel about yourself. If you walk around with your head down, you have a tendency to feel down. You are telling the world that you lack confidence, and that can signal to people that you are a target, that you will let stuff by you. It's a simple body language that exposes what you truly feel inside. If you're feeling down, you tend to look down. You'd be amazed at how changing your body language, lifting your head up, can give you a whole new perspective on life. You start to see things much differently, and it will begin to affect how you feel. It has to. You're no longer staring at the ground, at your problems, and not feeling good about yourself.

It's harder to feel bad with your head held high.

A queen, a woman with self-esteem, handles adversity with grace. Even when her world is crumbling around her, she never lets her crown fall. Life will put you through plenty of tests and throw many obstacles your way, but it's how you pass those tests, how you overcome those obstacles, that distinguishes you as a queen.

Think of Jacqueline Kennedy Onassis. Remember those pictures of her at President Kennedy's funeral, holding the little hands of Caroline and John-John? Just days before, she had witnessed the assassination of her children's father, her husband. She could not have felt anything but a pain too immense to put into words. Yet there she was, giving strength to the entire country. She had a pride and a will to represent something higher than herself. She was making a statement for others. She was a champion. And in many ways, she was the closest thing this country has ever had to a queen. She is remembered not for her extreme wealth and jewels, nor for her exquisite taste—although that was very much a part of who she was—but for her grace in the face of adversity, for her generosity and charity. And for always holding her head up high.

Another woman who held her head up high for the nation was, of course, Dr. Betty Shabazz. She is also a queen. As the wife of Malcolm X, she stood by a man whom many believed to be a negative force in this country. His was not a popular stance. But she was there for him. She was there when their home was firebombed. And she was in the front row at the Audubon Ballroom in Harlem when he was gunned down. She used her body to shield her four little girls, while pregnant with twins.

After her husband's tragic death, she carried on. She

got her master's and doctorate and raised six girls alone. She never let anything stop her from becoming the woman she was born to be—a true American inspiration. Even after her death—in a fire set by her grandson in 1997— she remains a figure of dignity, honor, and royalty.

A queen never sells out. She will sacrifice quick money and material goods for the greater purpose of keeping her soul. She may take three jobs to take care of her two kids when Daddy's money ain't coming through, and she doesn't complain.

That was my mother, Rita Owens. She laid the foundation for me to become a self-proclaimed queen. She made the ground fertile for me to persevere, no matter what the obstacles, and to keep my head up. My mother always told me how smart, beautiful, and talented I was. In her mind, there was nothing I couldn't do. When I wanted to learn the drums and guitar, she paid for lessons. When I entered talent shows, she sat in the front row. When I played basketball, she was there, cheering the loudest. And when I got into trouble and started running the streets, she talked with me, and she prayed for me. She never limited me. My mother believed in me before I even believed in myself. And because of that, no one can shake my confidence now.

I know there are many, many young women who don't have a solid picture of what a queen is because there isn't one in their lives. But even if you don't know a strong mother—or a grandmother, a tough aunt, a straight-talking teacher, or an encouraging neighbor who can be your champion—you can still be a queen.

It starts with you. You have to want to be a queen. You have to want it for yourself. You have to know yourself.

I know who I am. I am confident. I know God. I can take care of myself. I share my life with others, and I love— I am worthy of the title Queen.

So are you.

PART ONE

...

LIFE

1

■ ■ ■

A QUEEN CREATION

Latifah was born when I was eight years old. It was the late 1970s, and Muslim-sounding names were popular all over the country, but especially in Newark. My friends called themselves Malik, Rasheedah, and Shakim. Everybody had a Muslim name. Winki went by "Jameel."

Maybe it was the spillover from the riots or the resurgence of the popularity of Malcolm X and the Nation of Islam among young people that gave rise to the new nomenclature. Perhaps it came from the black revolutionaries and the Black Panther movement that defined civil unrest in Newark neighborhoods. I think people were looking for a sense of self that went beyond what they thought society had to offer.

For me, *Latifah* was freedom. I loved the name my parents gave me, Dana Elaine Owens. But I knew then that something as simple as picking a new name for myself would be my first act of defining who I was—for myself and for the world. *Dana* was daughter. *Dana* was sister. *Dana* was student, friend, girl in the 'hood. But *Latifah* was someone else. She would belong only to me. It was more than a persona. Becoming Latifah would give me the autonomy to be what I *chose* to be—without being influenced by anyone else's expectations of what a young girl from Newark is supposed to be. Or what she is supposed to do. Or what she is supposed to want.

My cousin Sharonda had a book of Muslim names, with the meaning listed next to each one. So Sharonda and I went through the book to see if we could find something for us. Sharonda picked *Salima Wadiah* for her names. *Mamoud* was already her last name. So she became Salima Wadiah Mamoud. We made up a little song, a chant for her name: "Sa-lim-a, Wa-di-ah, Ma-moud—rocks the house! Sa-lim-a, Wa-di-ah, Ma-moud—rocks the house!" We used to bug off of that all day. "Sa-lim-a, Wa-di-ah, Ma-moud—rocks the house!"

Then it was my turn. I was excited, turning the pages of the book. There was *Aisha*. Pretty, but not me. *Kareemah*. Cool, but common sounding. Then I got to *Latifah*.

Sharonda's father, my uncle Sonny, was a Muslim. He had a younger daughter whose name was Latifah. I thought that name was beautiful. I loved the way it sounded, how it just rolled off my tongue. So I was already feeling that name, but when I read what it meant, I knew that was me. *Latifah:* "Delicate, sensitive, kind." Yeah, that was me.

Even though I played kickball, basketball and softball, climbed trees and fences, fought boys, whipped their asses, and was big for my age, "delicate, sensitive, kind" accurately described exactly who I was inside. I loved the name. I loved the meaning, and I loved how it made me feel— feminine and special. The people in my world may have been perceiving me as something else, but inside I felt delicate, sensitive, and kind. I knew who I was inside, and I wanted to show a bit of that on the outside—with my name.

The "Queen" didn't come until a decade later. My first single, "Wrath of My Madness" was released before I actually signed with Tommy Boy Records. The 45 just had "Latifah" on it. When it was time to sign a contract, my lawyer asked me what my "p.k.a." or "professionally known as" name would be. When I rhymed, I called myself the Princess of the Posse, because I was one of the only women in my clique. I was thinking about calling myself MC Latifah or Latifah the MC. I even thought about just leaving it as Latifah, but it was too plain, just out there.

Around this time, the late 1980s, the conflict in South Africa was coming to a head. Nelson Mandela was still imprisoned, and the United States was pressuring companies to divest their interests in the country that made *apartheid* a household word. My mother and I would get into deep discussions about the plight of the South African women and talk about how segregation and racism were alive and kicking right here—in the very country that was opposed to apartheid in a nation halfway around the world. My mom and I revered those African women we didn't know, because they seemed to be so close to the most royal ancestors of all time. Before there was a queen of England, there were Nefertiti and Numidia. The African queens have a unique place in world history. They are revered not only for their extraordinary beauty and power but also for their strength and for their ability to nurture and rule the continent that gave rise to the greatest civilizations of all time. These women are my foremothers. I wanted to pay homage to them. And I wanted, in my own way, to adopt their attributes.

So "Queen" seemed appropriate. Queen Latifah. When I said it out loud, I felt dominant. I was proud. When I said "Queen," it was like saying "woman." *Queen* became synonymous with *woman* for me—the way every woman should feel or should want to feel.

Queen is the ultimate woman.

When I told my mother what my new name would be, she rolled her eyes. "Queen?! How are you going to call yourself *Queen* Latifah?" She couldn't see me as a queen—not then, anyway. Maybe she thought *she* was the queen; therefore, I should be the princess. But queen? Nah.

But true to form, she just said, "Okay, whatever" and let me go with it. She didn't dig it at first, but she got used to it. When she would come to my shows, Digital Underground, the Jungle Brothers, and Public Enemy knew my mother as "Queen Latifah's mother." She became like the Queen Mother. And before long, she started to like it.

In many ways, she was the queen who gave me the guts and the confidence to become one myself. She gave birth, physically and spiritually, to Queen Latifah.

MAMA GAVE BIRTH

TO THE SOUL

CHILDREN

My mother and father sat us down in the living room of our Schley Street apartment for a family meeting. Winki and I could tell it was pretty serious because of their long faces. It was 1978. People were still wearing bell-bottoms and sporting Afros. Earth, Wind & Fire was the group of the year, and my brother and I didn't have a care in the world. That was before we were hit with a bombshell.

"Your father and I are separating," my mother said. "When two people stay together for a long time, sometimes they have problems. And sometimes those problems can only be worked out separately."

"It has nothing to do with y'all," my dad said. "I will be there for you. Your mother and I just need some space apart."

Together, my mother and father made the perfect couple (from all appearances). They were like Cliff and Clair Huxtable. They hardly ever argued (at least not in front of us), and they didn't fight. We seemed like the perfect family—mother, father, brother, sister. We even had a German shepherd–mix mutt. Even after they broke up, my mother never dogged out my dad and he didn't dog her out. They had respect for one another. That was important for me and Winki to see.

A lot of women break up with their men and get hysterical. They put down their children's father in front of the kids—or worse, right to the kids. But what these women fail to realize is that saying something bad about the father of your children only makes you look bad. And it has a horrific effect on kids. While you're tearing down your ex, you're also tearing down your children in the process.

To us, our dad was basically a good man and a good father. He was a big teddy bear who loved roughhousing and ball games. He was a man who was always looking for a way to have fun. He was the disciplinarian, but he was never too harsh. He was our protector and our teacher, and we loved him.

We could not imagine that we would no longer be a family. Separating? Okay. To my eight-year-old mind, it sounded like something temporary. A little space could be a good thing, they said. All I heard was "little." It wasn't sinking in. I was thinking that Pops would still be just down the hall.

The next thing I knew, my mother, Winki, and I were packing up and moving out.

At the time, I didn't understand what was happening. I just knew we were leaving. I didn't blame anybody, and I didn't take sides. Mommy was still Mommy and Daddy was still Daddy, except he wouldn't be there with us. But now that I am a grown woman, I realize that what my mother did took a lot of strength. My father was messing around with drugs and other women. His thoughtlessness and lack of self-control were hurting her and endangering her children's sense of right and wrong. He was jeopardizing their security.

Although she still loved him, she left.

If you are being dogged by a man, you can't stay. You've got to go. The longer you stay, the worse you feel about yourself. You are allowing someone to take a part of you without giving back. You end up with less of yourself.

It took a helluva lot of courage for my mother to leave my father. She was alone with two small children. She knew that if she left my father, she couldn't count on a steady dime from him; she would be in charge of earning a living. She ached and felt miserable. But she sucked it up. She had lost her own father just a year before. Now she was losing her husband and her marriage.

Although my mother was devastated, she did not stick around simply to be able to say that she had a husband. Facing the reality was more important than keeping up appearances. She did not want to live a lie.

Leaving had to be one of the most difficult decisions my mother would ever make. She had given up her entire life for my father. She had been accepted to Howard University and Spelman College. But instead of accepting a place at either school, she married my father. She left her comfortable home in Virginia to move "up north" to a cold, rough city of cement—Newark, New Jersey.

That was a major adjustment for my mother, a country girl, a military brat from a large family where things were taken care of. Now she had to do the caretaking. She was the middle of the seven children—the youngest girl—of Catherine and Henry Bray, an army sergeant. They lived on an army base in Arlington. Her backyard was Arlington Cemetery. (She told me she used to wake up every morning at five A.M. to reveille.) Her parents were protective. They wouldn't let her hang out much, except to sing with her sister Angela, whom everybody called Angel. That's how she met my father.

He was a soldier in the Honor Guard. On the base, they had a little service club where young people could go and chill and sing and dance. One afternoon, my father and some of his buddies were in the club's piano room singing Temptations and Four Tops tunes. My father had a little singing group called the Grand Prix Machine, and they were doo-wopping to "I Only Have Eyes for You." My mother and Aunt Angel came in and asked if they could do backup. Mommy was sixteen, and she didn't even know the song; it was before her day. But she improvised. By the time they were done singing, "I Only Have Eyes for You" became my parents' song. And my mother was in love.

Actually, back then, it seems like my mother was in love every week—but always from afar. She was one of those dreamy girls who longed for adventure and romance. With my father she found it. He was a big, handsome, chocolate man with thick, wavy hair. He had this cool pimp strut and a smooth way of talking, with an "up north" accent and Newark slang. To my mother's young, tender, Virginia ears, it must have been like hearing jazz for the first time. Breezy and sweet and sultry.

She was swept off her feet. She thought he was the most fascinating and most exciting man she had ever met. Little did she know until she got to Newark that just about every guy up north talked that same talk and walked that same walk. But she was sixteen and in love. You couldn't tell her anything.

She left her friends and family in Virginia and married my father. A year later, she had my brother, and two years after that, she had me. She wasn't even twenty years old, and she already had a husband, two babies, a new town, and a new life. She had taken a chance, and it was the bridge between girlhood and womanhood. The next big chance she took was leaving my father. He was taking her womanhood from her. She had two choices: Stay and be less than she was, or leave and, even though it would be lonely and hard, be the woman she knew she could be.

Our life wasn't easier without my dad, but my mother never let us know how tough things were. She just took a couple of extra jobs and handled her business. Winki and I didn't want for anything, and she found a way to keep us in Catholic schools. The only dramatic change was moving, that just after moving to our beautiful garden apartment on Leslie Street in Hillside, we had to abruptly move once again. This time it was to the Hyatt Court housing project a few miles away. Until then, our family had always been moving to a better place and a better neighborhood—I had known four different apartments before I was eight—but this time, it wasn't a step up, and Daddy wasn't there.

The project consisted of brick buildings, three stories high, in the East Ward of Newark. The three buildings formed a courtyard in the center where people always hung out. My room, on the third floor, looked out onto the courtyard. I was fascinated watching the people, listening to the music, the arguments, the dogs barking, the kids playing. There was always activity out there, no matter what time of night.

Winki and I did a lot of growing up in Hyatt Court. So did my mother.

Our first year there—I was seven and Winki was nine—we were playing down the street from our building. As we were heading home, we saw this guy on the corner, drinking. I don't know what I was thinking, but I said something smart to the man like "You old drunk!" and started to run. But the man was a quick old drunk, and he grabbed my arm and shook me. I broke loose and ran home crying, with Winki right behind me, and told my mother what happened.

My mother was a small, slim woman. She had never had a fight in her entire life. But I know one thing—my mother knows about adapting. She would sneak people, because you wouldn't look at her and think "fighter." When I told her what happened, I saw her transform into a mad superwoman.

Her eyes got wild. She turned off the stove where she was preparing dinner, rolled up her sleeves, and stormed out of the house and up the hill. We were trailing behind her, breaking into a sprint just to keep up. She found the man on the corner and walked right up to him. She stepped just inches from his face, dwarfed by his brawn and height. Standing on her toes, she got right in his face and wagged her finger at him.

"Do you speak English?" she barked. He nodded.

"Does she look familiar?" she said, pointing to me. At that moment, the lightbulb must have gone on over his head, because he started explaining.

"She said some nasty thi—" he tried to get out, but my mother held up her hand to quiet him.

"I don't want to hear it," she said. "If you put your hands on either one of my children ever again, I will kill you."

And she meant it. We knew it and he knew it. She turned, grabbed our hands, and stormed back down the hill. I had never seen my mother flex like that before. But when it came to her children, she didn't play. She wasn't about to let anyone mess with us.

When all else is crumbling is when you have to call up that fighting spirit. That day my mother taught me that sometimes you have to stand up and fight for yours. She was a quiet fighter. The best fighters aren't the big bullies with the muscle but those who just make it happen every day with no fanfare or bravado.

They just do what they have to do to survive.

Part of that fighting spirit was manifested in the way my mother set up our house. Rather than using her energy to be angry at our surroundings, she worked extra hard to make sure our apartment became a home.

Outside it looked like any other inner city: the barren

steps leading into the complex were caked with soot and grime; the halls and courtyards filled with noise and craziness every evening, especially in the summer; horns blared up and down the street. But when you walked inside Apartment 3K—you were in Owensville.

She placed a small bowl of potpourri on a little table by the front door. When you walked in, the first thing you noticed was its sweet, delicate smell. Throw rugs graced every floor. Mom had style and could whip up a joint with no money. She found brightly colored fabric at a discount store and threw it across the couch in just the right way. She sewed pillows for the living-room chairs. She made curtains. The apartment was spotless.

My mother wanted 3K to feel like our space. With so much change in our young lives, she knew just how extra important it was for us to feel comfortable and safe. She wanted us to come home to a place where we would have dignity in our surroundings. Respect for our living space was on the path to having respect for each other and ourselves. She created an environment where we could come together at the dinner table every night and look around and say a prayer for the abundance we had in our home. We would focus on what we had inside, not on the barren landscape that made up Hyatt Court.

Winki and I each had our own room. And we were allowed to decorate it the way we wanted and establish our own styles, too. Winki's room was filled with Tyco racing cars and tracks. There wasn't much room on the floor to get around, but he didn't care. He had a shrine to auto-motives. His prized possession was a big Pisces poster on his wall. He was a true Pisces—moon, rising, everything was in Pisces.

My room was bare. I put my bed, on top of which was my collection of dollies, against the window, which over-looked the little courtyard. I had a tea set and table in the corner, and in the center of my room I kept my stereo—an eight-track player—and my favorite music. The open space was perfect for dancing around.

My mother's presence went with us everywhere. That was how she was. Every house we lived in was a castle. She spoiled me. To this day, having the right space is one of the most important things to me. When I'm in Los Angeles, I have to rent a house. But I still find a way to bring my style and level of comfort to it. I make sure I have candles and in-cense. I fill the house with pictures of my mom, my brothers and sister and friends, to let me know that home is home.

There was no shame in living in Hyatt Court. Yet a dishonorable mentality *is* bred in the inner city. My mom was determined to have us recognize the lack of consid-eration for one's neighbors, the dearth of ambition, the hopelessness, and the resignation that seeped into many of the people who had lived there for years and who had no intention of ever moving. My mother's fourth job was to keep us from buying into the negativity that flowed through the hallways and up from the courtyard and that was knocking on our apartment door.

"Just because you're living in the projects, doesn't mean you're *of* the projects" was one of the first things my mother said to us when we moved to Hyatt Court. For her, it was not a permanent home. She saw low-income housing as a great stepping-stone for people who are struggling to get on their feet and who are working toward a goal, as my mother was. She had plans to attend and finish college so that she could get a good job and we could have better. And she expected the same thing from us.

"Look, you're black; you're already at a disadvantage," she said. "You have to work twice as hard to make it. So don't get comfortable here." That was her big fear: that rather than seeing Hyatt as a means to getting someplace better, we would come to feel that we belonged there—forever.

Although my mother had little choice about where we lived during the school year, she made sure we spent part of our summer vacation down south in Maryland and Virginia, where her family had a big house on a beautiful piece of land. There our life slowed down and was cleaned up. We ate from fruit bushes and pecan trees that we climbed. There were pools with clean water where there weren't a thousand kids crammed in to get a splash like at Newark's pools.

People smiled and had manners. All of my cousins down south answered "Yes, ma'am" and "No, sir." There was church every Sunday. And every meal seemed like Thanksgiving—no leftovers there.

When we returned home at the end of every August, we were reminded that we were different from the other kids on our block. We had just come from a summer of activity and friends; it wasn't enough for us to just hang out in the courtyard. Instead of finding trouble on the streets, we were more interested in *fun.* We took advantage of a rec center across the street. Winki and I would play cards, Uno, Trouble, Monopoly, Ping-Pong, Connect Four, and Othello. We knew we would find happiness and safety among all those games. There was no temptation to be out in the courtyard—because that was just hanging out doing *nothin',* and if there was one thing we were always looking for, it was entertainment. Looking back, we barely noticed that we lived in the projects.

My mother used to organize field trips for the building. We would take bus rides to the museums in Manhattan, the Bronx Zoo, Wildwood Park, and the Jersey Shore. She knew it was important for us to get out of our environment. Kids need to go beyond the boundaries of their neighborhoods—whether it's Hyatt Court or Park Avenue—and see something different from what they wake up to every day, even if it's only a park in a different neighborhood. My mother wanted us to look out the window of the bus and to see that the world was a big place with lots of opportunities. She wanted to expose us to the open doors that were out there for us.

My mother got off the late shift at the Newark post office at seven A.M. She came home, made breakfast for Winki and me, and took us to school. From there, she went to wait tables at the Holiday Inn at Newark Airport. She got off at two P.M., which gave her enough time to pick us up from school and then go home and cook dinner. She seemed tireless.

When she had classes at Kean College (now Kean University), she would scoop us up and take us to class with her. On some nights, a woman who used to clean the classrooms would take us on her rounds so that my mother could concentrate on her class work. Everybody on that campus knew little Dana and Winki. They loved us. We got candy and treats and collected balls from the field after lacrosse practice (we had never even heard of lacrosse until we started going to Kean). They were bigger than baseballs and thick and heavy, with tons of bounce, and we would put them in our pockets and bring them back to our neighborhood to play.

After class, my mother would grab a few of hours of sleep before getting ready for her shift at the post office. I think she averaged about two or three hours of sleep a day for an entire year. But she saved up enough money to put a down payment on this cute little light blue house on Central Avenue and Twelfth Street in Newark. It wasn't anything elaborate, but it would be ours, our first home.

She had the down payment; all she needed was a $40,000 mortgage from the bank to get it. They rejected her because she lacked a credit history. But she didn't let that discourage her.

She promised us when we moved to Hyatt Court that we wouldn't live in the projects forever. So when she didn't get the house, she moved to plan B (you always have to have a plan B). She found an apartment on Littleton Avenue, a nice residential area of Newark, where I spent most of my adolescence. We had the second floor of a three-family house, and it was like a palace. We had huge rooms and a big backyard.

But there was still something missing—Daddy.

My mother began dating around this time. Although she was very careful about bringing men around the house, she did, on occasion, invite someone over for dinner or back to our house after an evening out. One night, Winki and I were in my bedroom. There we discovered a small hole in the wall that led to the living room, where my mother and this man were sitting on the couch. The hole didn't go through the wall, so being nosy, I took a steak knife and dug through the wall to the other side—to the living room. The hole was big enough to see everything. Winki and I took turns looking. My mother sat on the couch with this guy, and they were talking; then he gave my mom a deep kiss.

Nothing more, but my brother and I were hurt. He wasn't Daddy. What was he doing getting so close to my mommy? It was like our world came to an end. When my parents split up, my mother told us, "Mommy and Daddy are separating." She didn't mention anything about other men. "Separating" meant that they were taking a little break from one another but that they were still together. Right? Winki and I were not thinking about divorce, so what was this guy doing kissing our mother?

When he left, my mother came into my room to say good night, and my brother and I were sitting on my bed in tears, upset because we saw our mother kissing a man who wasn't our father. Snot was flying; we couldn't catch our breath.

The first thing she noticed was the hole in the wall. We were in trouble for breaking up her nice new apartment. And we were in trouble for being nosy. But my mother talked to us. She explained that she was a single woman and that it was okay for her to have dates. She needed to go out and enjoy life, too. She didn't leave that room until she knew we understood what she was saying and that we were cool with it.

She wasn't confrontational. She just knew it was important to talk things out and let us know that she was more than just Winki and Dana's mother. She was also Rita Bray Owens—a woman with her own desires, interests, and needs. As young children, of course, Winki and I did not think of her in any other role than as our mother. We needed her to explain to us that there was another side to her that was not about mothering and raising us but that was about being a woman. Needless to say, she rarely brought anyone home after that.

It is a luxury, in some ways, for children to be able to think of their parents as only parents—not as everyday people who struggle with work, money, relationships, or any of the other things that fill the hours and minds of every adult. Winki and I did not have that luxury. Discussing these big issues—from dating to scraping together the money to move to a better house—made me and Winki, in a funny way, our mother's peers. Of course, she was still a parent who could lay down the law just by raising her eyebrow, but we also had a relationship that was based on her communicating with us as adults about everything that was going on in her life. It made us grow up quickly and smart.

I became resilient.

Now it takes a lot to really get to me. I don't trip out over little things. I pick my battles. You can spend only so much energy on trying to control what other people do, or you won't have any energy left for things that are truly important. I could not prevent my mother from wanting to be with other men (nor should I have), and I could not make my father stop his philandering or flirting with drugs. That day, on the bed with my mother and Winki, I learned, although I didn't realize it at the time, that the only person in my life I can control is myself. I can't make choices for other people. And no other people—not even my parents—can totally live their lives for me. We can make choices only for ourselves.

And that's plenty of responsibility for one person.

DADDY'S GIRL

My dad was a Newark cop; a Vietnam veteran; a karate expert; a good-looking, smooth, all-around tough guy. Remarkably, he was not a chauvinist. He believed that women should have the same opportunities as men and that, given those opportunities, were capable of achieving the same levels of success. He put that seed into my head.

Lancelot Owens grew up in a large family, and his best friend was his older sister, Alita. She looked after him and protected him. So he grew up knowing that women could be strong and self-ruling and that they could take care of business. He saw that Alita's independence could take her anywhere she wanted to go. She was a queen—with 'tude and her head held high. He knew that if trouble came Alita's way, she would probably be okay.

So it is no surprise that my pops wanted to make sure his daughter knew how to take care of herself, too. He didn't want to have to worry about me.

I wasn't segregated, relegated, separated, or prevented from doing things just because I was a girl. I did it all. About the only person who wasn't always happy about it sometimes was my brother. My father took me everywhere he took my brother. He didn't separate us, as many parents do with their boys and girls.

Winki and I were privates in my father's army, and he taught us how to be self-sufficient and prepared for this world. He wanted us to know how to survive—whether we were in the inner city or the inner wilderness. My father, a Newark boy, had to survive two and a half years in the swamps and battlefields of Vietnam. He knew firsthand the value of being prepared for every situation.

I was six years old—too young to have any of society's notions that girls are not tough—when my father took me, Winki, and our cousins camping for the first time at the Delaware Water Gap, straight up I-80. It rained the whole weekend, but my father made us tough it out. "Hey, life's not always going to be sunshine every day," he said. "What are you gonna do when there are a few clouds? You have to keep going."

We helped him pitch a tent and set up camp. He wanted us to experience the reality of the outdoors. Our bathroom was the woods, and my dad cooked over an open fire. One day he made us dehydrated eggs. The next day we had cereal with no milk. We learned to appreciate Frosted Flakes with water. He woke us up before dawn so that we could see how the sun rises in the east. He traipsed us through the woods, teaching us that moss grows on the north side of the tree. We learned (the painful way) how to identify poison ivy. We smoked out insects.

Because I lived in Newark, certain aspects of nature were unfamiliar to me. But my mom and pops gave me the chance to see beyond our concrete jungle, to find out that nature was something that needed to be both respected and conquered, and to understand how what I learned out there could be applied to our regular life. In the woods, I learned to live with very little. At times, it was harsh to stay in a tent with a bunch of guys, but there was also great glory at the end of the trip, just in knowing that I had gone days without running water or a roof over my head. I felt tough and proud.

I came back home curious about what else was out there to be mastered; I wanted new challenges because I knew that when I surmounted them I had an incredible feeling of achievement and self-love.

■ ■ ■

My father, like my mother, also taught me how to be a queen. He gave me his love with hugs and kisses. And he taught me that I could be strong without being a bully. He taught me that it was okay to be a good guy. And he taught me that there was nothing that I couldn't do.

When I was with him, I climbed trees and jumped fences. When I came home all scraped up with cuts and bruises on my knees, arms, and elbows, he didn't try to make me stop. He would tease me instead: "Your legs are too pretty to have those marks on them," he'd say. "We'll just have to get them fixed." I didn't care about those scrapes, because I was having fun. And more than that, they told the world that I had been out braving peril. Those "marks" were the mark of a girl unafraid.

My mother had her role. She was the talker, the nurturer. And he had his. He brought out my fearless, aggressive side; he filled in the blanks of my personality. And it was like a harmony. Before my parents separated, they complemented each other when it came to raising us kids. I needed the balance of my mother's strong yet gentle manner that was always encouraging me and my father's no-.b.s., always-pushing-for-more attitude. Together my parents laid a solid foundation for both my brother and me. I didn't realize how much I needed both of them until he wasn't there. When we left our father, it was difficult not only for my mother but for me and Winki, too. There was a hole in our lives.

Our father was our protector. He was our hero, and we idolized him. He was the strongest, the smartest, the best-looking man in the world to us. There was nothing he couldn't do. He was Superman.

When I was about seven years old, my parents took me and my brother shopping in downtown Newark for school clothes. As we were driving home, we passed a corner where a man was yelling at a woman and pushing her around. Then he started slapping her. That's one thing my father wasn't down for. He taught my brother never to hit a female. "Only a punk will raise his hand to a woman," he'd say.

I knew we weren't going anywhere as long as this woman was getting roughed up.

And with the pressure of his kids in the backseat, yelling, "Daddy, do something!" my father got out of the car, pulled his gun, and yelled, "Freeze!" He threw the man up against the fence and frisked him. This gave the woman enough time to get away. When it was clear that she was safe, Daddy lectured the guy about being a real man and how he shouldn't be putting his hands on a woman. And then he let him go. My father wasn't on duty, but that didn't stop him from getting involved and doing what he knew was right. He spared that woman a beat-down, and he defused the situation.

That's the way I like to think of my pops—as a super-hero.

But there was another side to my father that shook my confidence in men. Although he was good at keeping up appearances, inside he must have been a mess. He carried around pain and torment from his years in Vietnam, where he shot and was shot at every day for two and a half years. When he returned from war, it was not to a hero's welcome. Later he joined the Newark police force, where, over the course of fifteen years, he killed several people in the line of duty and was never brought in for counseling. I know that he felt incredibly alone. Who of us could understand what it must have felt like to kill another human being or the reality of "kill or be killed"? He had issues, and he turned to drugs to numb the pain and to women for the love and confidence he could not find in himself.

Unfortunately, he was not the only one hurt by his bad habits. Winki, my mom, and I suffered with him—and for him.

Although Winki and I knew that my father had a few lady friends, we did not know until much later that he had also fathered children with some of them. "Weren't we enough to keep him happy?" Winki and I wondered. "He needed something better?" No matter how irrational these thoughts may have been, nothing stopped them from running through our heads, tearing away at our self-confidence. But something else happened, too, when I learned that my father had made babies with other women while he was still with my mom—my respect for him faded. And that loss was more difficult to accept than the fact that I had a half-sister who was just two years younger than me.

Michelle is twenty-six, and she never had a relationship with my father; she met him for the first time when she was seventeen years old. I also have a sister Kelly, who is thirteen, and an eighteen-year-old brother, Angelo. I love them all, and I know my dad loves each of his children. But what effect did his leaving his kids have on us?

I cannot speak for Michelle, Kelly, and Angelo, although I know from our conversations that they share my disappointment in our father. But my father's irresponsibility and infidelity left *me* uncertain about how I felt about men. Would every man be like my father?

For the longest time, I didn't trust men. When it came to being a father, Winki vowed never to be like Daddy when it came to family. He said when he got married and had kids he would never leave them. Winki had a plan: Between the ages of eighteen and twenty-two, he would play the field and have his fun. Between ages twenty-two and twenty-five, he would start looking for a woman he could spend the rest of his life with. By thirty, he wanted to be married, with at least one child. Unfortunately, I grew up during the "playing the field" part of his plan, so I watched as several different women came in and out of his life. And I saw the pain he caused them. Winki was solid, steady, and consistent in his love for *me,* but he was still a player when he was young. Were all guys dogs?

I've never really talked to my dad about what he did to our family and to his other children. I wrote him a letter in which I asked him why he went out like that. I told him he needed to grow up and stop living in the past. "Look at the future and the beautiful kids you've produced and be something. They need you. The world is tough enough; kids need their fathers." But I never sent the letter. I was too angry, and it seemed like a futile gesture. What I needed was to sit down with him and have a long talk. We needed to communicate. Wasn't that Mom's magic way? But I knew that before I confronted my father, I had to get my rage in check. No conversation is productive if it is all fire and brimstone. I had to arrange my anger in my head and know what I wanted to say to my father, or else I would just end up crying and screaming and storming away. My friend Monifa helped me put my feelings in perspective.

Her father had passed away when she was about nine. When I told her that I felt burned when I learned that my father had run through all of these women, she said, "At least you have your father."

She was right. At least he was still around; he was never far away. When I called him, he was there. When my mother was being stalked by an ex-boyfriend, my father went after him, and he left her alone. My aunt reinforced

Monifa's perspective. My uncle left her when my cousins were young. He was never there for them. They ended up addicted to drugs when what they really needed was their father's love and guidance.

Monifa and my aunt were hinting at the fact that as long as my dad was around, we still had an opportunity to try to fix our relationship. We are young with many rich years ahead of us. For the longest time, though, I felt like I didn't need my father. Hadn't I gotten along just fine without him? I was hurt.

But Monifa's and my aunt's words kept coming back to me. Although his leaving my mom did hurt the family, I know that his separation from my mother did not arise out of dislike for any of us but because he simply could not be a good husband to her. I accepted the fact that I could not control whether my father played around. Although I am an adult, I have decided that I do still need my father in my life. I looked at what I *could* control. I wanted to make a choice to have him in my life. I could decide to forgive him and to forge the bond that we hadn't had since those days when he and Winki and I went camping.

More than anything, I wanted to stop living in the past, because I could not change it. I wanted to steer the relationship into the future; I didn't want to spend any more energy getting it stuck in the mud of the past.

Control and choice. That's what it was about. I could control my disappointment that he was not the superman

I had built him up to be. And I could make the choice to accept who he was and to embrace the good that he *was* capable of offering.

I made a list in my head (which is what I do whenever I need to get something done) of the things I could do to bring us together again and to heal the wounds:

1. I can continue to make the choice to have my father in my life now.
2. I can talk to him regularly so that we never again lose touch with who the other person is.
3. I can start to see him as a human being, not as a superman who is always falling short of my expectations.
4. I can remind myself that as time passes, wounds heal.

Finally, I made the *choice* to love my father for who he is.

4

■ ■ ■

QUEEN OF HER
ROYAL BADNESS

The music was the lure. Funky beats I had never heard
before, brash words spoken in rhyme. Kids—dressed
in fly sweat suits, baggy jeans, and the latest sneakers—
dancers in the center of the floor, surrounded by crowds
forty and fifty deep. And onstage at any given night—
Grandmaster Flash, Dougie Fresh, Eric B. and Rakim, Salt-
N-Pepa, the Beastie Boys, Run-DMC, MC Lyte. This was
the Latin Quarters, the mecca of hip-hop in the mid-1980s.
And I was right there in the thick of it all, taking it in.

This was my education in the world of rap. For my

mother, it was Excedrin Headache number 9. I was definitely too young to be going to New York City all alone and hanging out all night. Looking back on it, I say to myself, "What were you thinking?!" I was blinded.

But in truth, I do know what I was thinking. Immediately, I was one with this world. My blood beat to its beat. Not only did I want to be there, I *had* to be there, and nothing was going to stop me. Not even breaking my mother's heart.

Rap was the newest music. Overnight, it seemed, rap had become the common language of youth. But it wasn't just music. It wasn't even just communication.

It was an expression, a culture, an attitude.

By the mid-1980s, rap was really taking off. The Sugar Hill Gang, with "Rapper's Delight," and Kurtis Blow's "The Breaks" cracked a hole in the music industry that has just gotten bigger and bigger with time. When I came onto the scene, rap was entering a new phase, with KRS-One, Public Enemy, and the Jungle Brothers. The consciousness movement was emerging. It was not just simple rhymes over the most popular songs; the music was about saying something.

Hip-hop transcended ethnic and racial lines. Young people were getting the chance to voice their opinion, and everyone—from the kids around the way to the mainstream public to the big white men at the record companies—was paying attention to it. And simply by being there, I was one of the people making the culture. It was amazing to be a part of such a force. We hit like the Coney Island Cyclone—just as wild and just as shaky.

The Latin Quarters was on the corner of Forty-eighth Street and Broadway. It doesn't exist anymore. A Sheraton Hotel sits on that spot now, thanks to the revitalization of Times Square, with its clean streets and family oriented stores and plays. When I was coming up, the Latin Quarters anchored what was a new and exciting world for me. It was vintage Times Square, with its funky movie theaters, peep shows, Playland, fake-ID shops, shady characters, and danger. I ate it up.

To get into the Latin Quarters, you had to stand in a line that sometimes wrapped around the block. The line was long because, before you even paid your ten dollar admission, everyone had to be frisked by security. I always felt violated, like I was being groped, but once I got inside I forgot about all of that. The doors of the club gave way to a huge open space. It was always dark, loud, and crowded. Even the bathrooms were packed. People were there just to say they were there. If you considered yourself a player in hip-hop, you had to be seen at the Latin Quarters. The rappers—many of whom are considered legends today, like Rakim and Run-DMC and Salt-N-Pepa—wouldn't just be onstage. They were also in the crowd, getting their dance on. Rappers infused the place.

■ ■ ■

The Latin Quarters wrote the Bible of hip-hop for me. I would bring the music, the vibe, the dances back to East Orange and to Irvington High. I was the first person around my way ever to do the "Rambo" and "wop." I was the wop queen. I put my posse down with the new culture from the city. I brought back underground tapes, with raps you couldn't hear on the radio. Every night, through the Lincoln Tunnel, I was transporting clothing styles and a new lingo that turned out to be more than a passing fad: a dialect that still sticks.

Back then, nobody really left Jersey that much. But I couldn't be kept away from New York. After my first night in Times Square, the pulse kept pulling me back like a magnetic force. I couldn't not be there. I was feeling the music, the dance, the language pulsating in me. My posse started to depend on me to bring them some New York flavor every week, and I loved going back to them, sharing what I had just seen. I was spreading the culture.

The other person bringing the flavor through the tunnel was Ramsey.

When I first started going to Irvington, hip-hop and the fashions now associated with it—the baggy, off-the-butt jeans; the boots; the oversized T-shirts; and the base-ball caps—were not the answer. It was all designer labels—Calvin Klein, Ralph Lauren, Polo, Gucci, Ann Taylor. Kids would be coming to school suited down. Some even carried designer briefcases. But Ramsey was a step ahead of everybody. He went to Greenwich Village to buy his clothes. Everybody in New Jersey was talking about "the gay Village," but Ramsey was there, scoping out the scene, collecting the look that all of Irvington High was trying to bite. He was the trendsetter. Ramsey was one of the first people besides me to hit the clubs in Manhattan. While most thought the place to party was Zanzibar or Club Sensations in Newark, Ramsey was partying his ass off in New York at the Palladium, the Garage, the Roxy.

Ramsey was bold. An immigrant from Liberia, he found himself catching up on his studies as a nineteen-year-old junior in his own apartment. There he cooked for us and kept the newest music, clothing, or news on the hip-hop scene right at hand. His place became our posse's home base. He was like a big brother sent from heaven. He became my second family.

Ramsey and I first crossed paths on the football field at Irvington High School. I was heading to gym class and he was coming from the field on his way to English class. I heard someone yell out from across the field, "Yo, Ramsey!" I quickly turned around to see this Ramsey dude.

For an entire year, all I ever heard was *Ramsey* this and *Ramsey* that. Ramsey, Ramsey, Ramsey. Sandy Hill, a girl I hung out with when I went to Essex Catholic, used to go with Ramsey. They lived across the street from each other. Every day I would get a complete, uncensored update on what they had done the day before. I knew everything about him, from the size of his penis to how well he treated her to what he had had for dinner the night before. He sounded so cool. Even his name was different to me. I didn't know anyone called Ramsey from around my way, and I couldn't forget that name.

So when I transferred to Irvington High School the following year, I couldn't wait to meet this Ramsey. I pictured him as a cross between Mandigo and Billy Dee Williams, the way Sandy described him. So I expected a great big beautiful hunk of a man.

But the guy who answered the "Yo, Ramsey" was this scrawny, rusty-elbowed, chocolate boy in a leather cap. His shirt was unbuttoned almost to his navel. He had on jeans and the latest Adidas shell tops. "That's Ramsey?" I said to no one in particular. I couldn't believe it, and I just started laughing. I went up to him, introduced myself, and said that Sandy Hill was my girl from Essex Catholic.

"She used to talk about you all the time," I said. "I know everything about you."

I had no intention of telling him exactly how much, though. But looks aside, Ramsey was everything Sandy had said. He was the man. He was likeable right away, and I could see why everybody loved him.

We clicked instantly, because he really knew music and hip-hop. He was down with all of the deejays. He was at every party and used to turn them out. When the music got good to him, he would rip off his shirt like he had mad muscles, like he was Arnold Schwarzenegger, and start dancing harder and harder, swinging the shirt in the air over his head. Everybody would crowd around him, chanting, "Go, Ramsey! Go, Ramsey!"

Ramsey knew all the deejays, but, ironically, it was my mother, the woman who died a little every time I went into the city, who put me down with the one deejay who would change my life.

In charge of activities at Irvington High School, my mother was responsible for getting deejays for the class parties. One day she introduced me to Mark the 45 King, a deejay who occasionally did gigs for Irvington. He was from the Bronx, where rap began, and he was a master on the turntables. He had done some work with the Funky Four Plus One More.

Mark and I hit it off right away. I started hanging out with his boys after school in his basement near the corner of Madison and Stuyvesant Avenues in Irvington. That was Jersey's Rap Central, where everybody was writing rhymes and trying out their shit over Mark's mixes. I started out as an understudy, just vibing. But Ramsey started pushing me to get in there and do my thing. "Come on, Dana, you know you can rock this jam." And of course, never-afraid-to-try-anything me grabbed the mike and freestyled. At first I sucked. But I knew that I had it in me. I could hear in my head the way I wanted to sound. It was just a matter of getting it from my brain to my voice.

Mark's basement was always buzzing with people from the neighborhood—and eventually we became a posse. I was the only female MC in the group and the youngest, so I called myself Princess of the Posse. Down there, in the small space among Mark's equipment, the world was far away and time ceased to exist. We were about the music. Only the music. And I had some great— and very patient—teachers. There was Apache, who had moved to Irvington from Jersey City. He was one of Mark's boys, and I thought he had the illest style. He had a deep, commanding voice, and when he rhymed, you just sat up and listened. He was the E. F. Hutton of rap. Latee was Apache's little brother (a rapping family they were), and he could mix up his styles. He rhymed slow and smooth like liquid, and he could bring the consciousness street rhymes. And there were other rappers like Lakim Shabazz, Lord Alibaski, Double J, Chill Rob G—one of the best freestylers ever. There were Shakim and Paul, who were brothers, who went to Irvington and whom I knew from school. They were hip-hop heads.

We had every rap album and every hip-hop magazine—all two of them. *Right On!* and *Word-Up* gave us the lowdown on who was releasing a record, who had just been signed to a deal. And *Right On!* filled in the blanks on the gossip tip. We wanted to know everything we could about the artists, the music, the clothes. We studied rap inside and out. Many of us eventually scored record deals simply because we were so prepared; we knew what we were getting ourselves into. It was like the training before the job.

Ramsey didn't rhyme or deejay, but he knew how to direct and critique and how to conceive ideas. We would sit there listening, giving the thumbs-up or a "nahhhh, that ain't workin' " for each other. And it was invaluable. We loved that. It was like being in rap school. Our goal then wasn't to get a record deal; it was to become good. We wanted to be tight. And we knew we had to be students first. Together we formed what later became the Flavor Unit—we kicked some ill flavor and helped make a name for Jersey in the rap game.

Ramsey was also the dreamer of the bunch. While we studied the hip-hop scene and practiced our music, Ramsey was filling our heads with grand notions that we'd all get signed to record deals and we'd make lots of money. Ramsey had the vision that we would make it big and that he would parlay that success into a business. We would have houses in Livingston and Short Hills—all near each other— and we'd have this mini-empire in New Jersey. In our spare time, we would build nice homes in the 'hood, fix up the parks, and provide jobs. Ramsey saw things for us that we weren't even thinking about for ourselves. He was the driving force behind our creativity. "Yeah, yeah, Ramsey, riiight!" we'd say before settling into practice. His vision was darn near close to 20/20. Many of us did go on to score record deals and make good money. I still plan on developing the 'hood, and I now have a nice house near Short Hills and Livingston.

Ramsey became my best friend.

The Burger King on High Street in Newark gave me the money to afford my hip-hop education. That's where I met Hakim and Bree. Hakim used to date a girl who worked with me, and he and Bree would always be in Burger King, hanging out, waiting for her to get off. Somehow we became friends. Hakim and Bree were taggers, or graffiti artists. Back in the day, it was real art, a phase of the culture that was another form of expression. It wasn't just putting your initials, or your tags, on a subway car; it was making a statement. I thought their art was cool, and I liked them. They were the ones who first took me to the Latin Quarters and introduced me to hip-hop.

We'd all meet at Burger King on Saturdays after I got off, around eleven P.M. In the bathroom, I would change out of my ugly brown, orange, and yellow outfit and into my hip-hop gear—a Swatch sweat suit (remember how they made clothes back in the day?), a pair of K-Swiss sneakers, some scrunchy Guess socks, a Benetton fisherman's hat, and either my Benetton or Swatch backpack, the one with the big clock on it. Everybody had a backpack. That's where I kept my Burger King uniform.

I was geared down; you couldn't tell me nothing. When the Burger King clothes came off, I put on a whole new attitude. The only thing I didn't have were the big gold bamboo earrings that were the thing. I couldn't afford gold. My brother had saved up for a nice gold rope chain, and we would alternate wearing that one chain. But I would never wear it to the city. I saw too many people get their chains snatched, either on the train or in the club. So I was content to be fly in my own way. I basically played it cool and watched a lot. I didn't come into the place like I was running it. I became part of the woodwork in the beginning, just observing until I picked up the style.

I couldn't wait for the live shows. It was like the Apollo of rap, where stars were made and broken. If you weren't good, you could easily get booed, no matter who you were or who you thought you were. And if you rocked, you got your props. Run-DMC and Kool Moe Dee would perform there on a regular basis.

It seemed like everyone wanted to be a rapper.

Ironically, though, I wasn't really thinking about a record deal. I was content to do my thing in Mark's basement. It was a hobby. I had my sights set on college. That's how I was raised. I ended up going to Borough of Manhattan Community College the following year, where I studied broadcast journalism. I wanted to be a newscaster or a lawyer. I liked the idea of trying a case in court, arguing before a jury, and convincing them that my side was right. Communicating, whatever the form, was my thing.

Hip-hop showed me another way to communicate, another way to reach people, another way to state my case.

I was at Latin Quarters when Salt-N-Pepa took the stage for the first time. I had never really seen a female group do their thing before then. They had a couple of hits, and "My Mic Sounds Nice" was blowing up the spot. They were fly girls who wore spandex and thigh-high boots and had all this hair. I was into leisure wear and sneakers.

It wasn't until Sweet T and Jazzy Joyce performed that I actually saw women rapping who looked like me. They were just regular girls in their Adidas sweat suits. They pulled back their hair in a ponytail, the way I wore mine sometimes. Not a lot of glitz, just straight-up hip-hop. Sweet T even rocked a fisherman's hat like mine. *They* were the first women to kill the Latin Quarters. Jazzy Joyce was one of the baddest deejays around, *and* she was a woman. Sweet T ripped the mike with her lyrics. They had the club in such an uproar that they had to come back the next night. We couldn't get enough.

I couldn't get enough.

For the first time, I saw the possibilities. I saw someone who looked like me doing something I'd only imagined doing in my sweetest, most distant dreams. Before Jazzy Joyce and Sweet T, it had never really occurred to me that

I could be up there, rocking the house. What I needed was a role model, and watching their success grow right before my very eyes put ideas in my head. My dreams were morphing into reality up there. I started thinking, "Maybe I can do it, too." Yeah. I could hear them: "Go, La-ti-fah, Go, La, Go! Give it to 'em, La!"

I could see it.

I went to Zanzibar and Sensations in Newark, but they mainly spun club music, and that was getting played out for me.

I was feeling hip-hop.

In addition to the Latin Quarters, there were underground clubs in Brooklyn, house and block parties in the Bronx, and hangouts in Harlem I would sneak off to. Sometimes the only person who knew where I was would be Ramsey. Sometimes no one knew where I was, including me. I was intoxicated by the scene.

One time I went to the city with Gloria, a girl I knew from around my way. She was about twenty-one. I always hung out with people much older than me. Not only was I big for my age, I was also mature. Gloria wanted to stop off at her boyfriend's place on the way to the club, and I said okay. Stopping over for a few minutes turned into an all-night affair, and we never did make it to the club. I was angry as hell. All I had was a dollar (she was driving, and she had said she would pay my way into the club), and the hours were ticking away. By midnight, I realized that I wouldn't make it home that night, but I was too scared to call my mother. With each passing hour, I knew my mother was growing more worried, and I was more and more afraid of the trouble waiting for me at the door when I arrived home.

Getting in trouble with my mother meant having her talk to you, which was worse than any ass-whupping. Even thinking about having to look into her eyes and explain myself was something I just didn't want to do. I'd rather play in highway traffic. I'd rather pull my fingernails off with a pair of rusty pliers. Anything was better than facing my mother when I knew I had done something wrong.

Usually when I went out, I would make sure that I was back in the house before anyone woke up. A lot of times, my mom and Winki didn't even notice I was gone. But this time, the sun was out and people were scurrying around before I was even heading home, and all I was thinking was, "That's my behind." I begged Gloria to take me home. And finally, around noon the next day, we left.

I tiptoed up the stairs and gently eased my key into the keyhole, praying that my mom and Winki would still be asleep on a sunny Saturday afternoon. When I opened the door, Winki was waiting for me. He blasted me: "What's wrong with you, Dana? Don't you know Mommy was up all night crying?" He was inches from my face, screaming. He wanted to knock the hell out of me. My mother had called all of the hospitals in the tri-state area, checked with all of my friends, the police stations, and even the local morgue. My brother was livid. He couldn't understand how I could be so damned inconsiderate. Me either. The night had just gotten away from me. I was so hell-bent on making it to the club—and then not getting found out—that I had lost sight of everything else. Especially my mom's feelings.

When I went to my mother's room, she hugged me. I thought for sure she would break down after all these years and whup my butt. But instead, she cried and repeated how much she loved me. I was crying, too. My mother was waiting for me, with understanding and a desire to listen, not with fists and harsh words. It blew me away. She said, "You're God's child and He will take care of you. Whatever you're out there doing, He sees you. You have to answer to Him.

"I just ask one thing: Please let me know you're all right. Just take a minute, call collect or whatever and just tell me you're safe so that I don't stay up all night worried, calling the hospitals and police stations. Okay?"

She wiped her tears, and from then on, my mother always knew where I was. That night, my mother taught me about real, unconditional love. She taught me about support. I couldn't explain to her why I was out there. How could I put into words my new obsession, the unexplainable force that drew me to hip-hop? But somewhere inside, she had faith in me, faith that she raised me right and that whatever I was doing would turn out okay.

She just knew that all my misbehavin' was going somewhere.

After a semester at Borough of Manhattan Community College, I told her I was going into what seemed like the craziest thing in the world at the time—the rap game. She said, "Go for it!" And I did.

Becoming Queen Latifah and a rapper didn't just happen overnight. Subconsciously I had been preparing for it most of my life. The music lessons. The talent shows. All those nights at the clubs, the endless hours in DJ Mark the 45 King's basement, the practicing, the reading, prepared me for something.

I didn't know the details of the world I was about to enter—I did not know how competitive, intense, or corrupt it would be, but I was prepared. Those wild days and nights, coupled with my upbringing—in a home that demanded excellence, where communication was number one, and where self-esteem was instilled very young—prepared me for just about anything.

Success is when opportunity meets preparation. All I needed was the opportunity.

LADIES FIRST

I was sitting in the kitchen of our apartment over the Modern Era Barber Shop on the corner of Halsted and Elmwood Avenues in East Orange. I was flicking between WBLS (107.5 FM) and WRKS-Kiss (98.7 FM). It was the summer of 1987, and DJ Red Alert on 'BLS and Marley Marl on Kiss had one of the best over-the-air music battles going.

You never knew who to tune to. If you listened to one, the next day your friends would tell you what you missed on the other station. We used to tape their shows, they were so good. So I'm chilling in the kitchen, and I hear the beginning of "Princess of the Posse."

> Baseline affect me
> My rhymes direct me
> Forgive the crowds, oh Lord
> They know not why
> They sweat me.

My record. My song. Me. Playing on the radio. I was so excited, I don't even remember whether it was Marley Marl or Red Alert who was playing it. I just ran to the window and screamed out, "My record is on the radio! My record is on the radio! My record is on the radio!"

Our apartment had windows on both Halsted and Elmwood Avenues. I ran from one side to the other, screaming down the streets, "My record is on the radio! My record is on the radio!" I'm sure I woke up half the neighborhood. But I didn't care. My record was on the radio. I hadn't even officially signed with a label. And they were playing my song on the radio.

My dream had been realized. Actually it was Ramsey's dream. It was his pushing and his money that got our crew out there. I was one of the last to get put down, but when I did finally come out, I came out blazing.

■　■　■

Latee got signed first, with Wild Pitch, one of the independent labels emerging in the rap game. That was a big deal for us, because we didn't know anyone personally from around our way who had a record deal before Latee.

Jersey wasn't really on the scene at this point as far as rap was concerned. You could go to a club and the MC would yell out, "Is Uptown in the house?" and there would be screams. "Is the Bronx in the house?" "Yeeeaaaaaaaah!" "Is Brooklyn in the house?" The place would go wild; there'd be barking and hooting and hollering. Brooklyn was always represented at every party. It was *the* place to be from. But when the deejay called out, "Is Jersey in the house?" there was silence. Every now and then a few brave souls would manage a weak "Yeah!"

When I started going to the Latin Quarters and other clubs, nobody wanted to admit they were from Jersey. But the Flavor Unit—Latee, Apache, Lakim, Chill Rob G, Lord Alibaski, Shakim, Paul, Ramsey, and I, the Princess of the Posse—helped put Jersey on the rap map.

Latee blew up the spot first with "This Cut's Got Flavor." He performed it at the Latin Quarters and rocked the house. We were all there. It was a milestone for our posse. Latee's being onstage was like each of us being onstage. He performed on behalf of the entire crew, and it was lovely. Next thing we knew, Chill Rob G also got a deal with Wild Pitch. Then Apache, who I thought was the best overall rapper among us, got signed and was doing a record with a guy from the Bronx. Soon their stuff was being played on the radio.

Then it was my turn.

DJ Mark and I went into Scott's Studio in Orange, New Jersey. Ramsey had given us $700, his rent money, to cut the demo for what would become "Wrath of My Madness" and the B-side, "Princess of the Posse." Scott's Studio was a rinky-dink place off Day Street, but it might as well have been the Hit Factory for all I cared. I did a little intro, "Greetings I Bring from La." I had gotten the beat from Jamaican rapper Half Pint. From the start, my style was different. I sang the intro and rapped in a Jamaican dialect. Nobody was doing that back then.

We did the demo in a couple of hours (we'd had a lot of practice in Mark's basement). When we finished, we were all smiles, because we knew it was good. The next day, Mark gave the demo to Fab Five Freddy, who was blowing up on MTV's *Yo MTV Raps*. Fab Five Freddy got a copy to Tommy Boy Records. And, within a few days, I got a call from Monica Lynch, president of Tommy Boy, who was head of A&R, artist development, at the time. I had just come in from a basketball game when the phone rang. Monica wanted to discuss a deal. She wanted to meet me. Me, Dana Owens, from around the way. In the past six months, I had gotten my high school diploma and a record deal.

I hung up the phone, ran into Winki's room, where he was napping, and jumped on him. "I'm getting a record deal!" I screamed at the top of my lungs as I tackled him on the bed.

Then I called Ramsey.

It was Ramsey's vision—not to mention his rent money—that brought success to the Flavor Unit. Ramsey just knew that we had talent—and he was unwavering in his conviction that I was going to make it big. He had more confidence in me than I had in myself. In my vision of the future, I saw college. I saw newscaster. Rap was a hobby. I saw lawyer.

Ramsey saw fame and fortune.

It's rare to have friends who want more for you than you do for yourself. Too often friends want to be top dog, or at the very least, they want everyone to be at the same level, fighting the same fight. But Ramsey wanted to see us all succeed. And he was willing to make sacrifices. He risked getting evicted. He ate mayonnaise sandwiches for weeks. He would do almost anything to find the money for us to get studio time so that we could perfect our demos.

Ramsey saw Queen Latifah even before I did. He was a seer—and a magician. Not just for the vision he had for all of us, but for the way he held our group together.

■　■　■

When I first started touring and doing club dates around the country, I had no clue about money: when to get paid and how to go about actually getting my hands on my take. My music career was careening ahead of my business savvy. Common sense told me that *I* didn't collect the money from the promoters myself. So with each show, I'd have a different person track down the promoters. In most camps, that person is called the road manager. But I wasn't that sophisticated yet. As far as I was concerned, I was still just a girl rapping out of someone's basement in Jersey.

Sometimes I would have my friends collect the money. Ramsey did it a few times, but his sense was more creative than business. Professor Griff from Public Enemy, with whom I did a lot of tours, took me under his wing and would do it for me when we toured together. But the more I toured, the more vulnerable I felt. After a show in Connecticut, I sent one of my cousins to pick up my money, about five thousand dollars, from the promoter. The promoter said something about the gate not being what he thought, and all he had for me was three thousand. But my take was not dependent on the gate. The deal was five thousand dollars, sellout or no sellout. When my cousin came back with the promoter's lame story, Shakim, who was chilling with me, volunteered to go get my money—all of my money.

I don't know what he said to this promoter, but he returned in ten minutes with every penny I was owed. I was not surprised. Shakim knew how to take care of business. I had watched him grow from the lanky boy in my geometry class who never showed up to a man who seized responsibility.

By the time we graduated, he could get any job done.

When we were in school, Shakim wanted to go out with me. I had to tell him, "Straighten up. I can't go out with you, man. You smoke too much." I didn't like that. "And you don't come to class enough to be with me." Nor did I like roughneck guys who weren't about something. If he wanted to be down with me, he had to get his act together. I didn't say that to make him come to class and stop smoking weed. I was telling him the truth because I saw something in him.

He did start coming to class, and he basically stopped smoking. We ended up becoming study partners. He got a B and I got a C (I'm still trying to figure that one out). He trusted me, because I was honest with him from the beginning. I liked the fact that he knew that he needed to make changes in his character and he did it. We never did get romantic: our friendship took over, and by the time I was hitting the road with my first album and making enough money that it needed to be looked after, I thought about Shakim helping me manage my career.

I put the notion into his head when he had a steady job. He seized the opportunity immediately, even though it was a huge risk. What? Trade a regular paycheck to help manage your friend's music career—something that might or might *not* take off? And we know what the odds look like for making a living making music. But Shakim did it. And he expanded his role to managing the whole ball of wax. He wasn't content with being just road manager. He wanted to prove that he could do it all. Shakim and I and my mom learned the business together. She held down the fort at home, communicating with us by phone while we were on the road. In just a few years, my record deals and regular gigs grew into a fine entrepreneurial business—Flavor Unit Entertainment, where we were managing other groups, too.

In Shakim, I have a great business partner. But I also have a friend to whom I can trust my entire life: from my personal, day-to-day dilemmas to my music career to my record label. He holds it all together.

I guess nobody ever told Shakim about himself before we met at Irvington High. But I knew from the start that he had the makings of a true friend. And true friends hold each other accountable. I did not see any other choice but to tell him to get his shit together. A true friend won't let a friend be self-destructive.

Tammy is that friend for me. She's the one who is always telling me about myself. She knows how to do it without saying a word, too. When I was in Los Angeles doing *Living Single,* Tammy came out to be with me: She needed a break from Jersey, and I needed a friend in that strange new town. I also needed a trainer to help me stay in shape. Tammy would be my trainer, we decided. I can be one of the most undisciplined people, and I wanted someone who wouldn't let me slide.

Tammy devised a postwork schedule for me. I'd come home from taping *Living Single,* be dead tired, and she would say, "Okay, Dana, let's go." I bitched and moaned as I changed into my shorts and old torn-up T-shirt. "Okay, give me twenty-five dips," Tammy would say. "Twenty-five dips?!" I'd start yelling. "You must be crazy. I've been working all day and you want twenty-five dips? What happened to warming up?! How about ten?"

"Give me twenty-five," she'd say in a calm voice.

I would curse her out. But she just stood there and took it, looking at me as if to say, "I'm waiting." I'd eventually do the twenty-five dips. And then two more sets of twenty-five. She wanted me working up to my potential. And what's more, she got *me* to want to work up to it, too.

When Tammy talks, I listen.

I met Tammy at Irvington High School, also. She was one of my mother's favorite students. My mom would come home telling me that I had to meet this girl. She called her Slammin', Jammin' Tammy Hammond. Tammy was the baddest basketball player, male or female, to step onto Irvington High School's court in the past decade. She was all-city, all-county, all-state, all that. I played a little ball at Essex Catholic, and I wanted to see if this girl was as good as everybody was saying.

I came up to my mother's school one afternoon to meet her. My mother had a meeting with the principal, and I was sitting in her seat in her classroom. Tammy came in and just looked at me as if to say, "Who are you, sitting in Ms. O's seat; get out!" But instead of saying that, her voice overrode her expression and she said, "Hello," friendly and strong. I told her who I was and that I knew exactly who she was. I challenged her to a game of one-on-one. She waxed my behind; I think I scored two points. And we became great friends.

From that day on, I would go over to Tammy's house a few times a week for dinner. Her mother, Mrs. Freeman, was always cooking. Dinnertime at Tammy's house was like Thanksgiving every night. There would be fried chicken, cornbread, greens, and my favorite—macaroni and cheese. Her mother could throw down in the kitchen, and the house, full with Tammy's three older sisters and older brother, was always alive with laughter.

I was one of only a few of Tammy's friends who were allowed to come over. Tammy's mom was strict.

Very few friends were allowed over to her house, and Tammy couldn't go out much, either. It was school, basketball, and church for Tammy. But Mrs. Freeman liked me. It was an honor that she felt good enough about me to make an exception to her rules. She became like my second mother. So Tammy was able to hang out with me without her mother worrying. Sometimes, she should have worried. Once, I convinced Tammy to sneak out of the house late at night after everybody was asleep. I got her to take her mother's truck and go to the city to party. And she did it. She was so scared. The whole night she stood in a corner, looking at her watch. "Dana, you're going to get me into trouble."

"Chill, Tammy." I tried to calm her. "We'll be home before anyone knows you're gone."

She did end up loosening up. A bit. She even danced a step or two. We left the party as the sun was coming up. Nervous Tammy drove practically ninety miles an hour to beat it home. She dropped me off, and she made it into the house before anyone missed her. We still laugh about that night.

We bonded. We were like sisters. My mother treated her like a second daughter. To this day, when I'm on the road a lot, Tammy will go visit my mother, and it's like me visiting my mother.

My friends are a blessing: Ramsey, Shakim, Tammy, GiGi. We've been tight since we were teenagers back in the day. They have been there for me through my success and through my rough times. But I think that having them in my life is more than just a gift from God. Just as I made a choice to repair my relationship with my Dad—well, I have also made a choice about the kinds of people I want to be surrounded by. I am not telling you here about the people who have dogged me, who have talked behind my back, or who fell by the wayside when I was still jammin' in Mark's basement making plans to go to college. I chose not to pursue those friendships. I felt something internally when I was around those people that was different from the way I felt around the Ramseys and Tammys. I felt defensive and edgy, not light and free. I watched my back. But with my true buddies, I could focus straight ahead. I was never self-conscious; I never held back.

When I am around my friends I feel *good*. I feel *secure*. Our friendship is based on something that is completely unspoken: trust. And that trust, combined with years of experiences together, has forged a bond of understanding and unconditional love. And that gives *them* the freedom to be truthful with me. They know that I might not like what they have to say—but they also know that I won't cut them off for telling me the truth.

I decided early on that it wasn't the number of people in my posse that counted but the quality of those people. I couldn't think, act, sing, or be myself if I were going to be with people who dug into me. Now, I am not saying that it was always easy to walk away from people. It's never clear-cut. Every life has people who amuse you with good times—on the surface—but who prick holes in your self-confidence by putting down your ideas or making off-handed comments that shoot right for your Achilles heel.

And just when you think, "Dag, I don't want to hang with this," boom, you end up going out dancing, sitting by the ocean, sharing some laughs. But what I realized with those people in my life was that a lot of the negativity stuck. And getting it unstuck took energy. The superficial fun wasn't worth it, because deep down I had been poked.

So I decided, early on, that if I was going to be Queen Latifah, feeling worthy and good about myself so that I could be my best, then I had only one choice about the company I kept. It would be only with the people who brought out the best in me. I had to lose the rest. It was not always an easy choice, but I am proud of it. Never do I find myself wasting time with people. Instead, I have the hours—and the head—for those I can count on for love and truth.

Tammy, Shakim, Ramsey—we are all royalty. And that's all I want to be surrounded by. Ramsey is my inspiration. Tammy is my conscience. Shakim is my anchor.

And they all have my back.

6

...

WHAT YOU GONNA DO?

> Thank you—as you—come back in—to the beat
> Give a shout out to my brother, L-A-N-C-E
> Up in heaven restin', chillin', watchin' over me
> You know you're too good to be forgotten
> Daddy's no longer here, but Lance is in the house
> There's only me and Mommy, you the man of the house. . .
> —"Black Hand Side," *Black Reign*

I n the early spring of 1992, my family and friends threw a big surprise party for my twenty-second birthday. I had a top 10 single, "Latifah's Had It Up 2 Here," off my *Nature of a Sista* album. I was nominated for a Grammy. And I had a little part in the Spike Lee movie *Jungle Fever.* I was having a ball. I traveled to Europe for concert dates. My albums were selling, and fan letters were pouring in. I was enjoying success. Miraculously, I found time to hang out with family and friends.

We were all coming up.

Ramsey and I shared an apartment in the Dixon Mills complex in Jersey City. Latee had just gotten his own place not too far away, and some of the old gang—Apache, Paul, Shakim, and I—got together to help old boy move. One of the last things we had to do was haul this heavy-ass couch up two flights of stairs. When we finally got it up the steps, we couldn't get the monstrosity through the door. We had to angle, stretch, strain, and maneuver for an hour. When we finally got the sofa into the apartment, we just collapsed on the floor, exhausted. Everybody grabbed a Heineken, laughing and trying to recuperate.

I got a page. It was a 911 from Ramsey. He worked at a video store a few blocks away from Latee's. I called him, and before I could get the "hello" out, he said, "Your brother had an accident on his motorcycle." I asked him if it was bad. "I think so," he said quietly.

My heart dropped. I couldn't think.

Winki was at University Hospital in Newark, and Shakim and I headed straight for the door. He drove. On the way to the hospital, it seemed like Shakim missed every green light. When we stopped for a red, my mind screamed, "Take the f---ing light, man! Let's do it!"

At the Pulaski Skyway, it started to rain. It had been beautiful and sunny all weekend. But now it was almost dark; the sky was getting low and stormy. All of a sudden,

I felt really funny, as if I were not myself. My brother and I have this spiritual connection—two Pisces, two fish traveling up and down the same stream. As the rain picked up, I got a chill, and my whole body shook.

I saw what looked like my brother's motorcycle on a tow truck at the emergency entrance to the hospital. The bike was twisted and mangled. "Oh, God," I thought. "Please let him be all right. Please let him have escaped this. Maybe he jumped off before it was too late. Please, God, please!"

I had bought him that motorcycle. When I got myself a Honda CBR600, it was so fly that Winki decided he wanted one, too. Never mind that he already had a bike. He was the one who hooked me on motorcycles, so I thought it was only poetic justice that he should have the phattest, the illest bike around.

When we were on the road together, we had a free, wild feeling that nothing else gave us—not music, not hip-hop, not even cutting loose with our buddies. When we took our bikes on the open road, it was our private realm. All at once, we were completely in control and then not in control at all. The power of the motor was under us, and only the wind was between us and the pavement. We were completely exposed. It was terrifying and exhilarating. Riding with my big brother, I felt like the queen of the roads.

Out there, no one could bother us. We were one.

■　■　■

My mother definitely didn't want Winki to get another bike. But true to form, ultimately she relaxed, and she, Shakim, and I decided we would surprise Winki, and we bought him that Kawasaki Ninja ZX7 for his twenty-fourth birthday. He was so surprised. Shakim then bought a bike, too, and before we knew it, we had a whole road posse. That spring, we rode all over New Jersey and around New York City. We planned to go to Belmar and Philly for the Greek picnic that summer and to Connecticut for a biker convention.

We had the road in front of us and our whole future ahead of us.

I never imagined that bike, bought in love, would be the cause of Winki's death.

Winki's boys were in the emergency room's waiting area. "Where's my brother?" I shouted at them. They just looked at me like they were going to cry. They led me to the family waiting room. It was a small space with muted browns and beiges, an old couch and a couple of chairs. My mother sat in a chair. She was eerily calm. I collapsed next to her, and she held my hand. "Dana, Winki's been in an accident," she said in a soft, slow tone. "He was hit by a car. His bike went under the car. All we can do right now is pray."

Nothing we can do? Just pray. I had never felt so useless. I panicked. Maybe I got a prayer or two off—but I was mostly begging, begging for God to spare Winki's life.

After what seemed like an eternity, a doctor came into the room. She wore surgical scrubs and looked strained, like she had something difficult to say. "I'm sorry, but we lost him," she said.

I looked up at her. "No, he's not dead!" I screamed through tears. "You better go back in that room and do something! Go back in there! You ain't telling me this crap! I'm not hearing it!"

Despite my barrage of anger and grief, the doctor kept her composure and explained what they had done to save Winki. "We cracked his chest and tried to pump his heart manually," she said. "We used eight more pints of blood than we would on anyone else. We knew he was a police officer. We did everything. But his injuries were too severe and we couldn't save him. I'm sorry."

My world evaporated. My mother started crying; then, like a faucet turned off, her tears stopped. The doctor said something about going back to prepare Winki's body so we could see him and say our good-byes. I walked out of the room and right through the hospital exit. Outside, I sat on the curb where the ambulances were parked and started crying again. I just kept screaming. I was in a state of utter disbelief and shock.

It would be months before I would finally accept Winki's death. Every morning and every evening, my grief pounded at my skull, tearing through my heart. Losing Winki was like losing half of myself.

I was numb and empty.

Winki was born Lancelot Hassan Owens Jr., but we just called him Winki. My mother said that when he was a baby, he slept a lot. When he woke up and tried to open his eyes, one always seemed to stay closed, making it look like he was winking. "You winkin' at Mommy?" my mother would say. "You little Winki." The name stuck, even after he grew into a big, confident man.

Winki was one of my best friends, but not because he was my brother. I know plenty of people who can't stand their brothers or their sisters, and that's a real shame. Blood doesn't necessarily mean connection or love or friendship. Even family relationships require work. Just because you're related does not mean that you're going to get along. You have to let everyone, even if they are your family, know how much they mean to you—with hugs, words of encouragement, and spending time together.

Winki and I did that all our lives. He always pushed me to be and do my best. He was the only man in my life who was there for me one hundred percent, who loved me unconditionally—no strings, no expectations, just straight-up love.

It was Winki's sense of adventure that helped me overcome a lot of the fear I kept bottled inside every time we moved, every time I had to switch schools and try to make new friends. Winki was the one constant friend in my life. Not only was he the man of the house after my parents split up, but he was also my protector and my soul mate.

Shortly after my parents' divorce, my mother took a rare vacation. She went to France with a group of friends for two weeks. We had to stay with my father's sister, Aunt Elaine, and our uncle Buddy, on North Fifteenth Street in East Orange. We were still in school, St. Aloysius, a Catholic grammar school in Newark near Hyatt Court. So my mother, aunt, and uncle worked out this schedule for us. We'd get up at six A.M., eat breakfast, and take the bus to Penn Station, downtown Newark, and the train to St. Aloysius. They gave us enough money to get to school, buy lunch, and catch the bus home. We had about five dollars apiece every day.

But Winki had other plans. He read the schedule and saw that we could catch a train to New York City. He decided we would play hooky. We had been to Manhattan with our parents plenty of times, but we didn't know the first thing about getting around the big city on our own. Yet that did not stop Winki. He saw opportunity and adventure.

"Let's ride to the World Trade Center," he said.

"Okay," said stupid me.

We took the train to the World Trade Center and went to the observation deck—more than one hundred stories up. We tried to blend in with a group of kids on a class trip. We still had on our St. Aloysius uniforms.

We walked around lower Manhattan, bought a couple of hot dogs with our lunch money, and then trucked back up to Penn Station in time to get home without arousing any suspicions.

The next day, Winki wanted to do it again. He was hooked on playing hooky. It was the first time either of us had done something so forbidden and gotten away with it. That thrilled us, but more than that, we felt independent. We were on our own, making our own decisions.

But by Friday, I was getting bored with our routine. I had seen all I could see at the World Trade Center. I was tired of eating hot dogs. And I really began to miss school. I missed my teacher, and I missed my friends. I told Winki I was not going to cut school anymore.

"I'm going anyway," he said. And he wouldn't get off the train at our stop. I was furious with him. But I stayed on the train. I did not want to go to school by myself—partly because I dreaded taking the train alone and partly because I knew I would have to turn us in and answer all of the questions: "Where have you been? Where's your brother?"

When we got home Friday night, the gig was up. The school called.

"Are Dana and Lance there?" the principal asked.

"Yes," my aunt Elaine said.

"Are they okay?"

"Yes. Why?"

"They haven't been to school all week."

That was our ass. Aunt Elaine was real cool, but Uncle Buddy wasn't to be played with. A big man from the Deep South, he had no problem tagging that ass. All he wanted to know was whose idea it was to cut school. I didn't miss a beat. I dimed out Winki immediately.

"It was Winki's idea," I said. "I wanted to go to school."

Winki got a whupping. And while I was listening to him holler, I was filled with rage. Who was Uncle Buddy to touch my brother, the one in charge of protecting *me*? I could not stand the thought of Winki having to take that beating. Buddy had no right to touch him. He should have waited until my mother came back. It was her place to handle Winki. Or Buddy should have called my father to deal with us. When Winki emerged from his whupping, I tiptoed over to his side of the room, and we dogged out Buddy.

That night we plotted again: We would call our father after everyone had gone to bed. We were seeking justice; the punishment may have fit the crime, but Buddy was crossing jurisdictions. Punishment was for immediate family to hand out, and it was humiliating to have to get it from someone else.

The next day, Dad had a nice talk with Uncle Buddy about putting his hands on us.

Once again, Winki and I felt like a team. He had my back, and I had his.

When he got older, Winki assumed the role of man of the house. He had an after-school job and would help Mommy out with household expenses. He even took it upon himself to give me an allowance—ten dollars a week. Fridays were payday for him and thus for me. I would clean his room for him and iron his clothes because I knew he didn't have to give me money, and I appreciated it.

I couldn't wait for the day when I could repay Winki. Becoming Queen Latifah and being a famous rapper wasn't my only goal. I also wanted to make enough money so that my family would never want for anything. By the time I was twenty-two, I was very close to that goal. I was able to afford a house, cars, clothes—and the kind of lifestyle we could only dream about as kids.

But even with a career that took me all over the world, making money, and making music that people were responding to, something was missing. I would go on tour, be back in town for a couple of days, and never get to see my family. I raced from one appointment to the next: promotional stuff, record-label stuff, business stuff, and stuff stuff I had to do. I'd stop at my apartment in Jersey City to sleep and be right back out on the road again. I never had a chance to get over to East Orange to see my mother and brother.

I decided I would buy a house and we would all move back in together. I had left our home in East Orange when I was eighteen and moved in with my dancers, Kika and Al, in Co-Op City. We had a bachelorette pad, perfect for my purple room, and some fly parties. Then I lived on my own for a little bit in a studio in Jersey City before getting a place with Ramsey. But I missed renting movies with Winki and my mom. I missed our family dinners that were full of laughter. I missed waking up in the morning and having breakfast with them before the craziness of the day started and we all went our separate ways. Although Winki and I were grown and had independent lives, I wanted us to be under the same roof.

I wanted my family back.

I looked for a house with zones, so we would each have our own apartmentlike space within the house. When we were growing up, my dad used to drive through Glen Ridge and Rosedale, and we'd look at the huge Tudors and colonials and dream about one day living in a big house like those. I looked at places in Montclair and Orange, in Seven Oaks—I wanted to stay close to home. Home was where my roots were, and I couldn't go too far. It kept me grounded.

I finally found a house in Wayne. One of only five other houses on the block, it was just a shell. The frame was there, the stairs were finished, and woods enclosed the backyard. But it was just an open house without amenities. That was perfect for me. I got to create and design the inside—I was going to customize this house. My favorite magazine was *Architectural Digest*, and I was really into fixing up houses.

It was contemporary and had great angles, skylights, and a big deck. And it was big enough for all of us to have our own space. My mother would get the master bedroom, of course. And Winki would have the basement when the house was finished.

After we closed on the house, Winki and I drove by one night, and because we didn't yet have the keys, we crawled in one of the windows. Winki used his big police flashlight, and we looked around our new place and imagined how we would hook it up. I had picked out a leather bedroom set—a headboard and matching nightstands—from a chi-chi store on Madison Avenue for Winki. It was modern and phat.

I got my mom an elegant burl-wood set that I had been looking at for two years in Beverly Hills. It was just her style. I was having a cherry-wood bedroom set built for my room. We came by the next day when the workmen were installing the jacuzzi, black and big enough for two. Winki was so crazy he got into it with all his clothes on, kicked back, and said, "Yeah! I will be macking mad honies in this!" We felt as if we were watching our dreams come true right before our very eyes.

I couldn't wait for us to move in. Between Winki's boys and my crew, the house would be alive all the time. I thought back to the way Tammy's house was always full of activity and laughter and imagined our house bringing me the same feeling of peace and joy that I had when I was with her family. We would have fun—and we would be a family again.

Not more than a month later, Winki was gone.

The last thing in the world I thought I would be doing was picking out my brother's casket. It was silver, with a white lining so soft it looked like clouds. Winki looked strong in it, wearing his police uniform and the haircut I always wanted him to have—a fade, squared off sharply around the edges. But his hands were cold. His eyes were closed. This was the most painful moment of my life. I loved him so much that I didn't want to live. If I couldn't share my life, my successes, my kids, my dreams, and my thoughts with him, it wasn't worth it. What good are gold records and money when you don't have your family around?

My brother was twenty-four. Dead? What are you talking about? It wasn't getting through.

At the viewing at Whigham's Funeral Home in Newark, I just sat on the little stoop in front of the casket, crying. I kept looking up at him. "Winki, man, how are you going to do this? How are you going to break out?" I talked to God: "Why couldn't you take me? I got to see the world a little bit. I got to do a lot of things—I'm cool to take this ride." Why Winki? He was settling into the Newark police force, where he already had a couple of commendations. He planned to marry his longtime girl-friend. He had his entire life ahead of him. It didn't make any sense.

The funeral was beautiful. The procession went on for miles and miles. It seemed like everybody in New Jersey turned up to say good-bye to Winki.

I was a mess for weeks after the funeral. I went through the motions of my life—waking, showering, phone calls—like a zombie. People were around, always bringing food and cards, and I spent a lot of time at Tammy's house. But as the days went by and people started going on with their lives, I was left with a huge void. I was weighed down with pain. I felt detached from reality and from people. Winki's absence shook me so far off my foundation that if I hadn't believed in God, I would have killed myself.

My first inclination had been to blame God. How could He let this happen? But Tammy wouldn't let me blame Him. Instead, she gave me space to vent and rode the waves with me. One night, we stayed up playing Stevie Wonder and a mixed tape of songs written by Gordon Chambers. I cried, I stomped, I kicked. One minute I was hitting walls, the next minute I was crying and so weak I could barely make a fist. I wanted to die myself. Tammy understood. She had lost her mother three years earlier, and she knew my pain. She said that when her mother died, the only comfort she could find was in the Bible. She opened the Bible and showed me Matthew 5, where Jesus said, "Blessed are the poor in spirit: for theirs is the kingdom of heaven. Blessed are they that mourn: for they shall be comforted." She told me that God does not make promises that He doesn't keep. We read the Psalms, and they gave me comfort.

She showed me things that other people had endured, like Job, who lost everything—all of his children, land— and God gave it all back. "And the Lord turned the captivity of Job, when he prayed for his friends: also the Lord gave Job twice as much as he had before" (Job 42:10) I didn't want to prosper; I just wanted my brother back.

I wanted to know if Winki was going to heaven. Tammy told me a story she heard from her minister. A woman lost her brother in a car accident. He was a hard-living man who smoked and drank. The woman had had a vision the night before the accident that her brother was in heaven making up the dinner table. He had on a pair of jeans and a T-shirt with a pack of cigarettes rolled up in one sleeve, his everyday outfit. In her dream, the man sent a message back: "Tell my sister I'm doing just fine."

Tammy didn't answer my question, but the story made me smile.

Deep down, I knew Winki was in a better place. Reality tells you everyone ain't going to heaven, but I knew that Winki had made his peace with God before he died.

He was a respected member of the Newark police force. He was getting ready to marry. His love for me and our mother was full of strength and humor. People wonder where their loved ones go in death. With Winki's passing, I became certain of something I had always been told in church but never fully believed: Our bodies are just shells; our spirits never die. But you need to know where that spirit has gone. With Winki, I know. He's in heaven, sending me messages that he's doing fine.

I worried about my mother. She wouldn't break down. She wouldn't really cry, just tear up from time to time. I knew that she was keeping everything inside and that her pain was just below the surface, eating her up. Her hair was falling out. "You have to be strong for your mother," people told me. That notion was whack because I couldn't even be strong for myself.

My father was a mess, too. The night Winki died, he came over to our place and sat at our kitchen table. "They took my chicken," he kept saying. "I dodged death a thousand times, but they took my chicken." He called Winki his chicken because he kept him under his wing. I knew my father felt like he had let us down. Here he was, a hulk of a man who could protect the citizens of Newark as a cop, protect this country as a soldier, but he could not keep his son from harm. He kept asking why Winki had to die instead of him. My father put his head in his hands and cried like a baby. A few months later, he sought help. He checked himself into the VA hospital to detox and to get himself together.

There was more to my father's despair than just the grief born of Winki's death, though. He felt guilty, too, because he missed so much time with my brother. At that moment, sitting at the kitchen table surrounded by tragedy, the same thing was going through all of our minds: You can never have even just one moment back.

Prayer, as much as I am ashamed to admit it, was not enough to keep me straight. I couldn't feel anymore— period. I was in a relationship, but I couldn't give, I couldn't love. My feelings were blunted, and I was blunted—literally. I smoked weed every day. I didn't want to deal. Every morning, before I even opened my eyes, I would be crying. Then I would stop, get up, and light a joint. Then I would put on my blue-tinted glasses and be ready. Or so I thought. I couldn't look at anyone without crying if I didn't have those glasses on. They shielded me from reality.

My days consisted of going to East Orange to see if my mother needed me, then driving over to the park to shoot hoops. The grief and pain flowed on the court, out of my heart, and through my hands to the ball. I would take shot after shot after shot. The tap-tap of the ball on the hot concrete slowly erased thoughts of Winki from my mind until it went blank. Then at the end of the day, I would go to the liquor store. I smoked and drank until I passed out.

Every day.

And every day, I wore those blue-tinted shades. If I had to look clearly at reality, I would break. So I kept the glasses on and got high and dimmed out the whole world. That lowered the volume on my feelings and then finally tuned things out.

This escape act wasn't helping me or my mother. As soon as my high wore off and I could focus, the problems were still there. Winki was still dead.

Winki had taught me that you have to face your pain and deal with it. Hoops helped me forget about Winki for a few moments every day, but friends and family—the people who lived life with me and Winki brought the most comfort.

My aunt Elaine, one of my father's eight siblings, was one of the key people in my life at that time. She had lost more than one brother. She seemed to have her life on track. She functioned and carried on. So I went to her and asked, "How do you get over something like this?"

Her advice was simple and direct.

"You don't ever get over something like this," she said. "You get through it. Over time you learn how to deal with the loss. But it's something you never get over, because you never stop loving that person."

Losing a loved one is like being an amputee. When you lose a limb, you still feel it, even though it's not there.

It itches and hurts. I can still feel Winki. It was helpful to think about him as if he were still here.

I had a contract with Motown to finish an album shortly after the accident, and I just didn't think that I had it in me. So I talked with Winki. And then I found that being around music and listening to the songs that Winki and I shared was therapeutic. Suddenly, my focus shifted. I poured myself into my music. I lived in the studio. Winki helped me write *Black Reign*. I became obsessed with finishing the album. It had become about survival.

The last cut on *Black Reign,* "Winki's Theme," was more personal than anything I had ever done. I had finally moved away from the weed and the monotonous beat of the court and found a way to release some of my pain. I put it into my music. "Winki's Theme" was one of the first songs that I really sang. That was me. And the music, a mixture of jazz, reggae, rap, the instruments—that was my soul.

I had to free my soul by releasing the pain through my music. It found an escape.

When I went on tour, some of the audiences knew the meaning behind "Winki's Theme." They knew where I was coming from and understood why I'd be in tears when I sang it. Often when I'd look out into the crowd, a lot of people would be in tears, too.

LADIES FIRST

This jam is dedicated to my brother Winki
Who is looking down on me from heaven
Watching my every move as usual.

There but for the grace of God
Do I go; do I go
There but for the grace of God
Do I go; do I go—go
I'm trying to take my time
On this rhyme
But it's bustin' from the seams
Like a fanstasy and eagerness of dreams
I'm moving all around
Oh, yes, I'm making leaps and bounds
There so much shit to say, no time to write it down
I'm skippin' to this and skippin' to that,
I've overflowed my cup.
I'm flowin' kind of quick,
I hope you can keep up.
Everything ain't cool just 'cause you slap me on my hand
There're things about me all of y'all have got to
        understand
Latifah—never was a teacher
Never was a preacher
Never was a saint
Never was conceited
Never been defeated
Sometimes I get tired, sometimes I want to faint.

But I never shut up when things piss me off
And if I got to curse at you to get my point across
That's what I got to do, that's how it's got to be
I've got an angel watchin' over me.

—"Winki's Theme," *Black Reign*

Black Reign was as much Winki's album as it was mine. He coproduced it. He was with me every step of the way. We made that album together.

Eventually I had to go back to work. Projects were coming my way. Movie offers were pouring in, and I started shooting *Living Single* in Los Angeles. My mother and I had been clinging to each other since the night of the accident. We were always worried about each other. So, when I left New Jersey, I called her every day. We were dependent on each other for reassurance that we were still alive. I knew that it was unhealthy and that we needed to start looking to ourselves for comfort, but we were stuck. I suggested that we see a psychiatrist for help in working through Winki's death. We had to get on with our own lives—independently. Or I would be the next to go.

I know that a lot of African Americans resist counseling. But I believe if something or someone can help you, you need to at least give it a shot. Why suffer unnecessarily when there might be some help out there? I never thought that there was anything wrong with seeking help from a professional to get you through a rough period in your life.

We didn't end up going to someone together, but I did see a doctor in California. I didn't need so much head shrinkage as an objective ear. The doctor let me talk and spill my rage without feeling guilty or self-conscious about it. And, little by little, the anger came out so it didn't fester, and time went by. I started putting the pieces back together.

My mother found solace in her art. She started drawing again; we turned the garage into an art studio. We would park the cars in the driveway.

Winki's death tested me. When we were riding our bikes around East Orange, I took our togetherness for granted. I felt immortal. The years in Hyatt Court were always with me, and I knew that what you have one day can be taken from you the next—I knew it in my head, but I didn't feel it yet in my heart. Why should I? Until the night I saw Winki's mangled bike in the hospital parking lot, I had never confronted loss. That night, I found an inner strength that I didn't know I had. I resisted it, because I just wanted to curl up outside the hospital and disappear.

But that inner strength was stronger than despair. In the face of death, I found the will to go on. Although I didn't realize it at the time, in those dark days I was living more than ever before. That's what living means—facing the music—whether it's bad luck and bad attitudes, failure, disappointments—or the death of the young man who was your brother and best friend. And living means letting go.

You have to let it go, or else you're going to go with it.

My aunt Elaine's words come back to me every day: "You don't get over it; you get through it."

One night, shortly after I arrived in L.A., I put Winki's bike key on a beautiful gold chain, hung it around my neck, and took my bike out onto Ventura Highway. It was two in the morning—open road—and the first time I had ridden my bike since Winki died. I desperately wanted another motorcycle ride with my big brother. I was still afraid of the loneliness that surrounded me without Winki, but I had to face my fears. And even more, I had to face myself.

I got on the bike, kicked it over, and took off. When I got up to eighty, I just let go. I screamed into the night, "Let's ride, Winki, let's ride!"

As usual, Mommy is dropping some science on us. Here, she's reading to me, age three, and Winki, five, in the park. Daddy took the picture.

I'm lethal with that karate stance—even at three years old.

Me at age two

Daddy and me on the boardwalk at the Jersey Shore in 1976

Lance and me showing off our guitar skills in 1979

I'm riding in style in front of Hyatt Court. And no, I don't have training wheels.

I'm leaning on my big brother. We're outside Hyatt Court with our bags packed, and with our cousins Tondra and Richie, heading down south for the summer.

I'm modeling the scarf, hat, and glove set
I got for Christmas when I was twelve.

Graduation day from the
eighth grade at St. Ann's.
I'm with my father,
brother, and paternal
grandmother.

The 1984 Irvington High School champion basketball team photo. I'm in the second row, third from the left. Tammy is holding her MVP trophy in one hand and
protecting herself from the coach's flails with the other.

Did I look nervous as I belted out Luther Vandross's "If Only for One Night" at the Irvington High School Talent Show in 1984?

Standing in front of the football field at Irvington High School, where I first met Ramsey

My best friend, Tammy, and me at our junior prom, 1986

That's the president (me, on the phone) and vice president (my mother) of Flavor Unit, handling business.

My dancer Kika and I have Tupac (then part of Digital Underground) in a girl sandwich. We were on tour together in Japan in 1990.

Performing in Japan

Giving our queen much love. Lance and me kissing Mommy.

My handsome brother doing a balancing act in 1992

Healing time. My mother poured her grief into this drawing, which she did for me after Winki died. (Finishing graphics by Floyd Simmons)

The original Phenomenal Woman, Maya Angelou, and I are chatting at Planet Hollywood in New York.

Celebrating my twenty-sixth birthday in Los Angeles

I'm hamming it up onstage at New York's Motown Café in 1998.

My father and me at the American Music Awards in April 1998

In front of Winki's grave (Motown Records)

■ ■ ■

JUST GET THROUGH IT

I'm sittin' alone—the queen with glimpses of thrones
My imagination takes to other places in God's creation
Sometimes I switch to jazz stations
To try to help my patience
Tested with stress from this crazy life I live
Nevertheless, keep my attitude positive

(chorus)
Life is what u make it, no matter how the cake gets
Or how high the stakes get, you got to take it
Some be on some snake shit, other futures are vacant
Or jake lit—those da thoughts that I wake with.

—"Life," *Order in the Court*

I was sitting in the middle of the pew, near the back of the
First Baptist Church in Nutley, New Jersey. It was
packed, as always. I wore my Sunday best, complete with

stockings and a pair of black pumps, and I wore that please-pastor-don't-stick-me-out-because-I-haven't-been-here-in-a-while look. This was the church I was raised in, and on this particular Sunday, I really needed to be there. Winki had been dead almost a year, and I still wasn't at peace.

I needed comfort.

The choir opened with "Precious Lord" and "Going Up Yonder." Then there was the offering and the message. Pastor Lawrence Roberts rose from his seat onstage and took the mike.

"Somebody out there is sad," he began. "Somebody is suffering. Somebody's in pain. Somebody is heartbroken." For so many months I had feelings that I couldn't put into words. I was still questioning God. I was still wrestling with the ways of fate, trying to figure out how and why my big brother, my strong brother, my heart, could be taken away for no reason. I was angry. I was sad. I was suffering, and I was certainly in pain. But when Pastor Roberts said, "Somebody is heartbroken," I knew he was talking about me.

You have to be able to identify what you're feeling before you can deal with your emotions. For the longest time, I didn't know I was heartbroken. But the instant I heard Pastor Roberts say it, I recognized it, and I felt a weight lift from me.

I'm at a place now where I can let go of my brother,

where I can miss him and remember him without feeling depressed. I'm ready to get through it, just as Aunt Elaine said. For six years, I've been holding on. Holding on to his memory, holding on to the pain, the sorrow, the guilt. And when you hold on to something too tightly, nothing else can get into your hand. You can't progress.

The only thing you can do with a tight hand is make a fist.

I wasn't moving, progressing. I was making movies, television shows, records, but inside, I was stunted. My relationships could only get so deep, because there was no room for another person. The memory of Winki took up most of the space in my heart. But now I am in the process of making peace, even in the chaos that often follows my life. Peace is a place where your soul is free, where you're completely at rest with yourself inside. It is a complete calm and contentment.

Being at peace is the only time you can hear the Creator. Where my mind can talk to my soul and my soul can talk back. That's where I find my center, that place inside of me that possesses the clearest and highest thought.

There are several different ways I create peace in my life. The first step is to be alone. Some people are afraid to be by themselves, and once upon a time, I was, too.

I was always surrounded by people. But I was still lonely, full of agitation, and looking around, thinking that there might be some better place for me to be, there might be people other than the ones I was with whom I should be going toward. Even though I was with people, I wasn't there. I wasn't *with* them. My mind was buzzing like a machine that keeps going through the motions but is only creating steam. I was so busy assessing my surroundings and the people in them that I was not dealing with me.

The only time you can deal with yourself is when you're by yourself. Then you can begin to think in an unobstructed way. Have you ever been in a room by yourself with your eyes closed and listened to your heart beat? *Solitude.* I even like the sound of the word.

The best place for me to be alone is in the bathroom. It is my favorite place. At least once a week, I turn off the television, unplug the phone, grab a book, some fruit juice, my CD player, and run a bath. I love oils in my bath—my favorite are Aveda. The gentle lavender and gardenia smells alone send me into instant relaxation. I melt into the water, the hotter the better, and let my mind roam. This is where I sort the wheat from the chaff: I go over the day in my head and think about what is important—and what isn't. I always find the same thing: The broken clutch on my car, the less-than-hot review of my new album, the five magazine interviews lined up for me in five different cities, are, as the title of the best-selling book says, "small stuff."

In that hot tub, behind closed doors, with the Wes Montgomery playing real low, I think about what I want to say to the world with my music. I ask myself what I did that day that I feel good about; I acknowledge whether there is something I would have done differently and make a private vow to change it next time. I set new goals for myself—whether it's promising not to call a man who is treating me as less than the woman and queen I know I am or committing myself to writing down that new rhyme that's been flying around in my head like a crazy bat.

I also find peace when I am alone with nature. I have to be able to smell clean air, see green, listen to the birds, feel the ocean ebb and flow under my big, bare feet. The greatest advantage of my place in Los Angeles is that the beach is right up the block. I can walk up the street, turn the corner, and squeeze the sand between my toes and listen to the waves. By myself.

During the making of *Order in the Court,* at a dark and claustrophobic studio in New York, I was so starved for some sand and salt water that after a night of mixing and remixing, I drove two long hours to the Jersey Shore. I walked along the crooked line where the brine meets the sand. I had to put my feet in that water. I watched the sun poke through the blackness on the horizon and rise above the ocean. I was alone. I could see my life from a distance— and see it clearly. And as I watched the water, heard the strong, smooth sound of those powerful waves, and saw that sun push its way up, I was checking in with God. Suddenly, the world wasn't weighing so heavily on me. I was reminded that I was just one person in the scheme of things—and that no matter what direction I went in (and Lord knows I was being pulled in many different ways), there was something bigger than me. It was late spring and cold, but I needed the connection—I needed to go outside of my life that day—away from the record company, telephones, producers. I had to be with just me before I forgot who I was.

After Winki's death, being alone became more than a luxury, something I would try to do when everything else was done. Instead, it became a priority. I was afraid more often than I had been when he was around, encouraging me and watching my back. I was afraid of failure. I was afraid of not being a good friend and daughter. I was afraid of being alone in the world. But how do you put this into words for other people? And what can they say? I turned to books. *Feel the Fear and Do It Anyway*, by Dr. Susan Jeffers, tells us to look our fear right in the eye and then turn our back on it and march up to doing whatever it is that we are afraid of. In a way, I had been facing fears all my life, but it was a great reminder to be myself. I even have my mother reading that book.

Conversations with God, by Neale Donald Walsch, is, like a dear friend, another important player in my life. A gift from Monifa, it answered so many of the questions I had about God. It's written in God's voice. "You cannot create a thing—not a thought, an object, an event—no experience of any kind—which is outside of God's plan. For God's plan is for you to create anything—everything— whatever you want."

Translation: You have the power.

More than anything, that book made me examine myself. It taught me that I could choose to wallow in my pain and grief, or I could choose to get up and get through it. The choice was mine. I couldn't blame anybody or expect anyone to pick myself up for me. Things happen. But what are you going to do when they happen to you?

I made a choice to live.

It came right back to the music. When Winki died, the song in me died. But I had obligations to fulfill. I was under contract to finish what later became *Black Reign*. You have to handle your business, no matter what you're going through. And, in this case, my business was making music. And it was a blessing. For most of my life, music has been my pathway to peace. I can get completely lost in a song. They say music soothes the savage breast, and that ain't no lie. If I'm wound up, stressed out, or bummed, I can throw on some Stevie Wonder or Teena Marie, and it will bring me back on track. Even after *Black Reign*, music continued to be therapy for me. I poured my grief into my music, into my lyrics, into my rhymes. I would sit in the studio—just me, the producer, and the mike—and listen to tracks and vibe.

I would take the tracks home with me and listen to them in my car on the way to and from Giant Studio on Fifty-seventh Street and Broadway. Once, I was driving into Manhattan and decided to take the scenic route through my old neighborhood in East Orange. One of my songs was blasting in my car. It was a beautiful, sunny day. I opened the sunroof and was basking in the rays. I drove past the parks where I played when I was a kid. I went through the Newark projects where we lived after my parents separated. Kids were out front, skipping rope and playing tag.

I felt as if the world had not changed, and I was comforted by all the familiarity. I felt grateful for my life. I started singing to the music:

Just another day,
Living in the 'hood,
Just another day around way,
Feeling good today,
Feeling lovely-eeah

Just another day,
Living in the 'hood,
Just another day around way,
Feeling good today,
I hear the [sound effect of a gun-
    shot], but I'm here to stay
    —"Just Another Day," *Black Reign*

By the time I got to the studio, I had nearly completed the song that ended up becoming one of my favorite cuts on *Black Reign,* "Just Another Day . . .":

> Well, it's a beautiful day in the neighborhood,
> A beautiful day in the neighbor-hood
> Can't go wrong, I feel strong and the flavor's good
> I'm with whatever comes my way,
> Hip-hop, hooray.
> Latifah's on vacation
> I'm just plain old Dana today

The music on that album is introspective. It was about me looking for answers, trying to find them in the music.

> Why the negative vibes
> Why do people take bribes
> I don't understand it, yo
> (I don't know)
> Why do bad people live and why do good people die
> Somebody got to tell me why?
> (I don't know)
> Why do people smoke crack
> Why do white fight black
> What's the scenario
> (I don't know)
> Why do hearts get broke
> Why do chumps get choked

They know I ain't no joke
(I don't know)

Now with the drums, to the bass, to the piano to the horn
It's a crazy-ass life and that's my word as bond
I'm trying to be as logical as I possibly can
But for the life of me, you know I just can't understand
What's going on some-times
Some situations like this come out in my rhymes
But Queen Latifah ain't going out just yet
When it comes to mastering confusion, I'm a vet.

—"I Can't Understand"

When I couldn't find the answers in my music, I had to find them in God. He became my last word. I rediscovered prayer while recording *Black Reign*. Now, I pray every day, but I don't go to God asking for a million things like "Lord, let me hit the lottery" or "God, please let me sell a million albums." It's not about that. When I speak to God, it's a release of my soul. Some mornings, I will lie in my bed and just start talking to God as if He were in the room with me—and of course, He is.

When I am alone in nature, in my tub, or in my bed waking up in the morning, that's my time with God, when I have my personal conversation with Him. And He answers me, through other people, through events. I have faith that God exists, and I never question it. It is one of the few guarantees in my life.

> Now faith is the substance of things hoped for, the
> evidence of things not seen.
>
> —Hebrews 11:1

Faith is the opposite of fear. It's confidence.

Everything starts with God. I know I can't make someone accept God, because you have to feel Him. But when life has taken a dive, I know how hard it is to keep the faith. Doubt is strong, and it has a sharp point that can pierce our soul when we're not looking. So when in doubt, just take the chance and say, "Okay, God, You do exist. Can You help me with this?" And He will. Start with the basics, and He will come in time. Things will happen for you. Whether Catholic, Muslim, Jewish, Episcopalian—no matter what your religion, faith is a universal healer.

If I don't believe in God, I can't have faith in anybody else, including myself. If I can keep my connection to God—keep my faith—I can conquer everything. I used to worry about so many things that were out of my control: Is my man being faithful to me? Is somebody spreading gossip, trying to hurt my work? Am I getting a fair deal? But I realized that I was spending time worrying—and being afraid of things—beyond my control. All of it was bigger than I am.

God will take care of that which I cannot command. I'll let Him fight my battles. I have faith that He will pick the right ones for me and that the rest will slip away, unnoticed, as they should be.

Being spiritual isn't about being perfect. The Lord knows I'm not perfect. To me, being spiritual is recognizing that we aren't necessarily operating on our own steam. And that ultimately, not everything in this life is under our control.

We have to let go and let God do His job. But first, we have to have faith.

PART
TWO

...

LATIFAH'S
LAWS

■ ■ ■

SPEAKING BLUNTLY

By the time this book is in your hands, I should be free from addiction.

My habit is cigarettes.

Being addicted to something, to anything, takes away your power. Here's what I mean: I hate smoking. I know that it's unhealthy. I hate the way it makes my body feel, the way it makes my clothes smell. It makes *me* smell. But I still want my smokes. I need them, and that need is beyond my control.

I hate having something control me like that.

One of the proudest moments in my life was when I quit smoking after my brother died. I wanted to cleanse myself. I spent so much time filling my body with alcohol, with weed, and with cigarettes that I couldn't feel a thing. Suddenly I was terrified. Nothing was coming in—not pain, not pleasure.

So I put it all down. I quit cold turkey. I encouraged myself with Post-it notes stuck up all over the house: YOU CAN DO IT, DANA! DON'T EVEN THINK ABOUT PICKING UP A CIGARETTE. COME ON GIRL, JUST ONE MORE DAY.

I knew it was one day at a time and that each day I didn't smoke was one day closer to quitting altogether. And I did it. It took a while for my body to adjust to not getting the nicotine it craved, but eventually, I started to feel great. My senses became alive again. I could smell more keenly and distinguish subtle tastes. My lips began to tingle. I could work out longer and breathe easier. I never realized how much abuse my body was taking from those cigarettes. I vowed I would never pick up another butt.

And then I lapsed.

I got a role in *Hoodlum,* and my character smoked. The movie was set in the 1930s, when everyone seemed to have a cigarette on her lips, and the director had me puffing unfiltered Winstons. I thought my chest would explode. But by the fourteenth take, I was hooked again. I was under the control of this little white stick of carcinogens.

■ ■ ■

When I was growing up, I thought it was so cool to smoke. The coolest man I knew—my daddy—smoked. In fact, I took my first drag from a cigarette I stole from one of his packs. I was four. My crazy brother woke me up one morning before dawn. It was still dark out, but as usual, any time of day was good enough for Winki's schemes. He was always figuring out something for us to get into.

He had gone into Daddy's pocket and taken a cigarette and a lighter, and we snuck into the den. He lit the cigarette, took a long drag, like a dummy, and started coughing his little head off. Luckily, the door was closed, and our parents couldn't hear him or smell the smoke. He then handed it to me. I took a little drag (but didn't inhale), so that I could be just like Winki. We felt like two very bad, very cool dudes. We were having a ball. We put the cigarette out, threw the butt out the window, put the lighter back in Daddy's jacket, and went to bed. And that was it—for then.

I never lost my fascination with smoking. In school, my homies and I used to sneak into the girls' bathroom to smoke. At first, there was the thrill of doing something grown up and forbidden. But then it progressed. I started to want cigarettes even when I was alone. I was getting hooked. That's the thing with drugs—you eventually end up wanting more: one, two, three packs a day.

I'm working hard to quit again. It's not so easy this time. Ever heard that once you quit something and go back to it, it's ten times harder to quit again? It's true. But I'm going to do it. I have to do it if I want to be free. I have to regain control. My family is helping. My mother won't allow any smoking in the house, and that definitely helps me because I don't want to disrespect her wishes.

If you see me on the streets with a cigarette, step to me. Because if there's one thing that people with an addiction need, it's accountability. If you hold me accountable (without being rude about it), like it or not, it will help me. I will know that I am not living in a vacuum where no one is watching my actions. Instead, I will realize that people have their eye on me, that they are holding me to my vow to be better. I don't want to let them down. And even more, I don't want to let myself down. It helps to know that people are out there rooting for you when you are in a rough game.

Cigarettes are my poison. I got hooked because I experimented once as a kid and it made me feel good. Next thing I know, I am pushing thirty and struggling to kick a habit. One thing that inspires me to quit is thinking about people who are addicted to other drugs and alcohol.

Tabs, mescaline, weed all came my way. And I had my stint with drinking and even cocaine. (I never tried crack and definitely didn't do heroin.) I often wonder how I was able to avoid getting hooked on all these drugs. Was it luck? Being at the right place at the right time? The part of my brain that I have in check and that sends vibes of willpower to the rest of my body?

No. It comes down to role models—good and bad.

My cousin Nikki has had a heroin addiction for nearly a decade. I've watched her get sick trying to kick the habit. Like anyone addicted to heroin, when she stops she is overcome with nausea, throws up, and her body chills and shakes. She then becomes addicted to methadone. She cannot function. She is powerless in the face of a drug. Nothing makes me more sad—or more terrified.

My father had a cocaine addiction. He was so dependent on scoring that he became obsessed. He'd be cool for a while; then he'd just bug. He wasn't abusive, but he just wouldn't be a great dad when he was on that stuff. Winki and I couldn't spend time with him because his priority wasn't always looking after his kids. You would think watching what my father did would be enough to make me never want to try cocaine. But I did.

A group of kids at Irvington High would come to school on Mondays talking about how "sniffed up"—high—they had been on the weekend. I thought they were losers, and I was not impressed. But one weekend, I found myself at a party with them. I was cruising the house and wandered into the kitchen, where there was a mirror with pristine lines of coke set up. People were just walking to the table, having a seat, and snorting up. I didn't see anything in there for me, so I went back into the living room.

I was chillin' on the couch when a guy in my class comes over and sticks his finger into my mouth and rubs it over my gums. He had coke on his finger. When I realized it, I snatched his hand away from my face. I couldn't believe someone would be so crazy. Everybody was cracking up, laughing at me. I was embarrassed.

But about twenty seconds later, the people around me started to fade out. My gums started numbing, and I was tripping. I couldn't believe the sensation. It was tingly and exciting. Suddenly, I wanted more.

I went into the kitchen and sniffed part of a line. At first, I thought I would gag. My eyes started to tear, but then, just like my gums, my nose became tingly, and it felt like it was wide open. I felt as if I could inhale an oak tree. And then I started to feel wonderful. I was a woman without a care in the world who could accomplish anything.

I understood—all too well—why people get hooked.

And I knew that night that if I ever did coke again, *I* would get hooked. And I knew what that meant: becoming obsessed, losing sight of what's important, and going broke—just like my dad. When I came down, the visions I had were not of being Superwoman but of becoming like my dad. I had the half-decent sense to know that those good feelings I had were really lies.

I gleefully accepted that the only way I would feel that kind of high was with God. And then it would last. I thank Him every day that I didn't get hooked.

■　■　■

I have lost a lot of friends who did not have a vision, as I did, that terrified them, and they became addicted to various substances. They could never feel how far was too far. They thought that they could handle anything, stay in control of the substances that were making them feel invincible, that were egging them on to cross any boundary.

The person who shook me the most was a girl on the Irvington High basketball team. She was a freshman when I was a junior starting on the varsity. She was so good that before the second half of the season, she had made it from the junior varsity to the varsity. She was the first freshman since Tammy to crack the starting lineup. This girl was talent. I remember watching her one day and thinking that she would definitely get a scholarship to play in college. A free ride. She was *that* good.

Before the season was over, she stopped coming to practice. Then she dropped off the team. After the season, I was walking to the Chinese food takeout joint on the corner of Avon and Springfield Avenues in Newark, and there she was, sprawled on the ledge of the store window— nodding. She was in a drugged stupor. It bugged me out. Here was a girl with so much potential: she was a great athlete, a kind person, and a beautiful woman. And there she was, sitting in the window of a grungy restaurant, like a mangy cat. The whites of her eyes had gone yellow and were half-closed, drool formed in the corners of her mouth, her head was bobbing.

I walked into the restaurant and said to her, "What are you doing? You are buggin'. You have got to chill with that shit!" I was half-angry, half-scared. One day she was a promising athlete, the next day she was a nodding addict. It was a slap to both of us. And I realized it could happen to anybody.

Seeing what drugs did to my father, my cousin, and to the kid from the basketball team deterred me from drugs. But there was even more that kept me from addiction: shame.

After experimenting with anything, the same trigger always went off in my head. I would think to myself, "Damn, if anybody found out I was sniffing coke, I would be ashamed." I thought, "If my mom or God knew, I would want to crawl under a rock."

But there was always another tug, pulling me in the opposite direction of what was right: curiosity. The thrill of doing something I was afraid of and not being afraid anymore. It was the same tug that got me up on the stage for the talent concert in elementary school. It was the same pull that brought me into the recording studio rapping my fast-beating heart out when I signed with Tommy Boy.

My one-day stint selling drugs was one of the scariest and craziest things I have ever done.

There was a dude from around my way who had the phattest Benz in the neighborhood. We all knew it as the mark of one very successful dealer. I used to see him driving around with his shiny racing wheels and tinted windows. One summer day, he was driving by my block with the windows down and his fine stereo blasting. He was at a stop sign, and I just went up to him and asked him for a job. I was seventeen.

My post was the corner of Avon and Twenty-first Street, starting at dark. He sent me customers, and I would exchange product for money. I stayed out there until ten-thirty and made $250. Quick money could become an addiction, too.

But for me, it just wasn't worth it.

I had just been elected president of Students Against Crack, an organization my mother started at Irvington High. I had to resign after I took the job with him. I told my mother I couldn't hold the prestigious office because I didn't have the time to devote to it, with school and basketball. The truth was, I was dealing. I couldn't stand being a hypocrite. How could I be out on the street selling and then in the school telling kids not to use?

Shame overcame me. I had to make a choice. I saw dealing taking me for everything—my dignity, control, independence. Those qualities, even at seventeen, were priceless to me. I left the dealer.

■　■　■

I rarely mention drugs in my music. I don't want any business glorifying the fast lifestyle that a lot of rappers promote when they talk about smoking blunts, drinking forty-ounce beers, and getting fucked up. I'm not down with that. My music is too powerful to put drugs into the mix. Yes, I experimented—and I came close to losing control, to losing myself with them. I was lucky—and I saw others who weren't.

I wish that the kids I see hanging out in the streets, looking for something to get into and who want to experiment, could see what I did. I see boredom on their faces, and I know that the quickest thing to take it away is going to be fast cash and the momentary thrill of a high. I wish I could put my cousin and the basketball player in their faces. But I can't. All I can do is put a message in my music about what it means to feel good—whether it's feeling sober or being able to taste the richness of chocolate and the spice of cinnamon when you're not on three packs a day. That's why I have chosen to make my music about being grounded, about treating yourself as royalty.

We always have an "it won't happen to me" attitude when we see other people making mistakes. Don't be fooled. It can happen to you—if you aren't careful, if you don't know who you are—anything can happen.

CHAPTER
9

■ ■ ■

''NO, YES''

Lesbian.
    That word seems to follow me lately.

I'm not afraid to do roles like Cleo, the hard-core, from-the-'hood, down-and-down dyke in *Set It Off.* I worked that role and I played her to a T. It was one of my most challenging parts. I am more proud of that performance than of any other. But it seemed that when that movie came out, everyone wanted to know, "How much of Cleo is really you?"

Do Al Pacino and Robert De Niro have to answer questions all the time about being gangsters? Does Jack Nicholson have to explain that he's not really the crazy man he portrayed in *The Shining*, *One Flew Over the Cuckoo's Nest*, and *As Good As It Gets*?

Even after the hoopla from *Set It Off* died down, the Lesbian Question wouldn't go away. So I thought I would demystify it—I'd make it a nonissue, and then what would there be for the media to chase? *Nada.*

I released a mixed tape before my album *Order in the Court* came out that was distributed underground. I cut the track "Get Off Mine."

Get off my dick / and tell your bitch to come here!

Okay, I admit—there was more behind cutting that track than just deflating the media. The hip-hop head in me needed to do something a little more hard core, a little edgier than what I'd been doing on my albums. Shakim came up with the idea. He said, "Yo, you should make a record like, 'get off my dick, nigga, and tell your bitch to come here.'" I liked that. It was in-your-face raw, and I knew it would get attention. Until then, I had kept my albums positive. But I was starting to feel too safe. Every now and then, I need to cut loose, play out a role musically.

■ ■ ■

There's still all kinds of speculation about my sexuality, and quite frankly, I'm getting a little tired of it. My ploy to get the media off track didn't work. It seems that in this country, sexuality is never a nonissue. Rather, it is always *the* issue. When there's nothing else to write about, when there's nothing else to say, everyone wants to write and talk about sex. It's a sure seller of magazines, air time. Albums.

But it's insulting when someone asks, "Are you gay?" A woman cannot be strong, outspoken, competent at running her own business, handle herself physically, play a very convincing role in a movie, know what she wants—and go for it—without being gay? Come on.

Can we live free from restrictions, boundaries, and opinions?

People fueled those rumors when I wasn't dating anyone. I felt as if I should run out and get a boyfriend, if only to say, "Look, I have a man, I'm not gay. Ridiculous." But I know better than to make a choice about my personal life just to make a statement to other people.

That's not me.

People are going to talk about you no matter what you do. So I learned I'd better just do what I feel like doing and leave the worrying to someone else. I follow my heart. If I want to chill in a gay club, that doesn't make me gay. If I dance all night in a straight place, that doesn't make me straight.

■ ■ ■

I want people to see me as someone who is proud and comfortable with who I am. I'm a liberal-minded woman who couldn't care less what anybody else does in their bedroom. That's on them. I want people to say, "Well, if Queen Latifah is hip to who she is, then I am going to be hip to who I am." Not "If Queen Latifah is gay, then it must be okay . . ." Or, "I can't mess with her."

Be secure in yourself. You don't need me—or any other public person, for that matter—to validate you. Not all the role models in the world can make someone proud to be something that society says is taboo, shameful. All we public people can do is set an example that shows how *we* can defy a label, how *we* are comfortable living out who we are. Neither I nor anyone else can make someone else's choices okay by extension. That wouldn't be fair, anyway. It would be a crutch. We don't live in her skin. Only she does.

I don't act the way society dictates that a woman "should." I am not dainty. I do not hold back my opinions. I don't stay behind a man. But I'm not here to live by somebody else's standards. I'm defining what a woman is for myself. Simply put, I am not interested in subscribing to what society has decided for half of humankind. I am an individual, and this is what I know: I don't like being a victim. I don't like being weak. I don't like being subservient to anyone. I hate to be taken advantage of. I've been to these dark places. And never will I go back to them. It's a fool who doesn't learn from mistakes. A queen uses her mistakes as a stepladder to climb higher.

And I've had a long way to climb.

Growing up, I was uneasy about my body. It was big. And, to make matters worse, I was uncomfortable with myself sexually. My father was basically a dog to women, and I watched my brother dog out a few ladies, too. I ran with a lot of guys, so, unlike many women, I was privy to inside conversations: "Yo, man, I did her last night and I'm going to do her friend tonight," as they laughed and slapped pounds. That's enough to make any woman gun-shy about getting involved. But every woman wants to feel feminine, and, well—like a woman. We are taught from an early age that the surest way to feel like a woman is to have sex with a man. Think of all the perfume and makeup advertisements that link femininity with the promise of sex.

For the longest time, I, too, believed that to feel desired and loved, to be in touch with my womanhood in all its entirety, I had to have sex. That was until I realized that I have the power to feel like a woman in a million other ways. I have the ability to say yes or to say no to a man and still feel like the big, beautiful queen that I—and every other woman—am. I control my own pum-pum, and nobody gets it unless it's on my terms.

That's a liberating mantra. One I suggest every woman adopt.

Since the beginning of time, we women have given men all the power. We've bought into the "There is a man shortage" shit and allowed men to think that *they* are the prize. Bump that. We women have the goods. They want to be inside of us where it's warm and wet and feels fine.

We have the power of the pum-pum.

Why not use it?* Make men come to us like real men. Yet we still allow ourselves to get used. I've been there, too.

The most major decision a woman can make is about who is worthy of sharing her body. Too many women think sex is the answer to every question and problem in their lives. They see sex as the only recipe for feeling beautiful and special; they believe that if they have a man they must be worth something. It's not so simple.

---

*Remember, though, that if you do choose to say yes, you have one more step to go—especially if you're single like I am:

> Brothers better strap their thang, thang, ladies
> Don't let a man if they don't have a condom
> —"Coochie Bang," *Black Reign*

There is no sex good enough in the world worth dying for.

My mother used to preach to me that my body was a precious gift. When I was twelve years old, she sat me down for "the talk." I was just developing a woman's body. My breasts were getting large, and boys were starting to notice me. My mother sat across from me on my twin bed in my room of our Littleton Avenue apartment, and we discussed her version of the birds and bees.

"Guys will try to have sex with you, Dana," she told me. "Your body is precious—the most precious thing you can give to someone. Make sure they deserve it. Don't give it to just anyone." That was rule number one. "That first time should be special, and it should be with someone you love. You should be married, but knowing how people are today, let me be realistic with you. If you have sex, make sure you're protected. Use, use, use protection! You have dreams, and you don't want to mess your life up."

My mother was on point on all fronts with that advice. I wish I had listened a little more closely to the things she said then. But, as always, I had a mind of my own. It was fueled by curiosity, and it ran on the thrill of doing something I knew was forbidden—and a little dangerous.

I met Raheem at Irvington High School. He helped coach the girls' basketball team. Sometimes he would drive me home after practice. That's how it started.

We were in front of my house talking. I was about fifteen. He was twenty-four. But we were having what I thought was a mature conversation. We ended up talking about sex, in the abstract, and before I knew it, we were kissing in the car.

And it progressed from there. Some days, I would cut school and go to his house. He didn't care about my education, that I was falling behind in all of my classes, or about my future. All he cared about was having sex with me. He told me all the things I wanted to hear. I was beautiful. Cool and smart. He made me feel like the bomb.

But all he was doing was preparing me for sex. Every time I went over to his house, all we did was have sex. After a while, I figured him out. I was being used. For Raheem, I represented an easy mark. He took advantage of my naïveté and my youth. He knew it was wrong. But he also knew he could get over on me. And aside from being guilty of being fifteen and thinking that I knew everything, I was also guilty of using him, too. I wasn't in love with him, but being with him was validating my womanhood.

I was just developing into a woman, but I wasn't quite there yet. I didn't know whether I was coming or going, and I said to myself, "I'm going to have it with the next guy who comes along." That, I thought, would push me over the line and into womanhood.

Along came Raheem.

But all that followed was shame and loneliness. I didn't feel special or feminine whatsoever. I was suddenly intensely aware of my body, but it seemed that I had lost some of my soul.

■　■　■

Basketball was a big relief that year. My emotions poured out of my body on the court. I channeled that energy into something positive.

We won the Essex County and New Jersey state championships.

I finally started feeling good again. On the court, during the finals, the shame lifted. In the mirror, I looked at my long legs. I examined my serious back. I took note of my firm breasts. I was pleased with my thin, strong fingers that could grip that basketball—and my long, powerful arms that could send it soaring up and through that damn hoop. That was a championship body.

That was the season that I learned rule number two: You can't run from a problem. When I found Raheem, I was running from my insecurity about being a young, developing woman. Suddenly—and puberty comes on *real* quick—I was no longer a tomboy, but a woman with broad hips and round breasts and an interest in having boys interested in me. I was also curious about sex. My problem was that I was caught between two worlds—that of the uninhibited little girl who could do anything and that of the young woman who was told by the world that she wasn't really a woman until she had a man.

Unfortunately, I was just too green to recognize my problem. I told myself that if I slept with Raheem I would be a woman. I would cross that line between girlhood and womanhood. Raheem seemed to hold all of the solutions.

Of course, in retrospect, I realize that I was rationalizing. Or more to the point, I was lying to myself, which is one of the worst things you can do. The first lies we tell are to our parents when we are kids: "I didn't break it." "I didn't eat the last cookie."

The second lies are the ones we tell ourselves. On the inside, we know one thing, but we convince ourselves of the lie on the outside—and act on that. That's what gets us into trouble.

Although I regained my self-respect after our championship season, I didn't wise up all that much about men later in high school. Guys pressured me a lot to have sex. They pressured me to the point where I would just give in and do it, because they begged so long and hard that it was easier to cave than to keep hearing their mouths.

One guy, Lamar, used to come around my neighborhood when we lived at 275 Halsted Street in East Orange. He drove this phat black Mercedes Benz. I didn't think he was cute and he was old enough to be my father. But he never drove through without finding me. He was always offering to buy me gifts. He wanted to take me to the mall and told me I could pick out anything I wanted. He would always ask me if I needed money. It started with flirtatious sweet talk, and ended with us in bed.

He was forty. I was sixteen. But I wasn't stupid. I knew he wanted something in return for his gifts. So when he gave me a fifty-dollar bill, I took it. I didn't need the money, but I just did it. As I lay in this guy's bed, looking up at the ceiling after we had had sex, I felt low. I was facing a depth I had never seen before. I had just been with a man I hardly knew and didn't like. For what? Fifty bucks. Once again, I wanted to feel desired—and there was something so adult and dangerous about Lamar. And that always intrigued me. But this wasn't cigarettes. And I didn't feel the wonder that coke brought.

My quest for thrills and quick fixes had finally gotten me. I couldn't shake this one. It was time to grow up.

Young or old, regret follows us through all stages of life. People rarely think about the consequences until after they've done something. We all wish we could take back an action, but we can't. I wish I had never slept with that guy in the Mercedes. I wish I had never peddled drugs. I wish I had never done a line of coke. I wish I had never puffed a cigarette.

But I did.

More than the acts, though, it's regret that attacks your self-esteem. Regret inevitably leads to our beating ourselves up. We start to judge ourselves and feel that we're stupid. Questions like "Damn, how could I ever have messed with him? What was I thinking?" spun around in my head like a scratched record. I went through it all.

Too many women, when they know they've made a mistake and can't fix it, stay right there. They wallow in that point and never move on. They beat themselves down so much that they don't get up.

Yeah, I made mistakes, but now what? Where do I go from there?

The pain and lowness—and loneliness—of all of my mistakes have been what made me want to change. You can only roll in the mud for so long. At some point you must get up, or else you'll stay right there.

There have been downsides—and major consequences—to each of my regretted acts—doing coke, selling drugs, and taking money for sex. But there's been an upside, too. Each experience reinforced who I wasn't—and who I *am*. Dana Owens wasn't the type to sell drugs on the street corner. She wasn't going to find herself balled up in a nodding, drooling, drugged-out stupor. She wasn't the kind of girl who sold her body for money. That wasn't me. And I had to put myself in check real quick.

I'd rather be broke than destroy my heart, than face the bottomless pit I did that night with Lamar. I'd rather have no money and hold my head up high than have drug money in my pocket. Every time you sleep with somebody, it's like you give that person a piece of your soul. Did I want this guy to have a piece of me? No.

Plain and simple. But it was a long road getting there.

LADIES FIRST

■ ■ ■

On *Order in the Court,* I have a song, "No, Yes," about choices—making a decision about whether to have sex with someone. It's got a simple moral to it: Think before you act.

I don't want to get too complex
'Cause the stress comes with the sex
I know you want to see me undressed,
You're fiending to taste my sweetness
And since I'm your sex interest,
It's about time for me to confess
I wanna smoke you like budda-bless
But my mind's like a bullet-proof vest
Is it no or yes?

My body's ready, my mind's blocked,
It's gonna take a lot to reach my hot spot,
I kid you not
I wanna set it and let you wet it,
So come and get,
And when we're through you'll need a paramedic
No never mind my thoughts dip
You might trip or flip and so instead I'm staying celibate
My body's ready, my mind's buggin'
So I'm strugglin' do I need your love or your lovin'
I just don't . . .

(chorus)
No, no, no
But my body keeps tellin' me
Yeah, yeah, yeah,
My mind keeps tellin' me
No, no, no . . .

—"No, Yes," *Order in the Court*

This rhyme is where I'm coming from today. I have to analyze each situation—no matter what my body is telling me to do—and think it through. Is this something I need to be doing? Should I have sex, or should I wait? And I'm an adult, a consenting adult, going through these changes. By the end of "No, Yes," I remain celibate; I don't buckle under the pressure from the guy or my own body. I just say no.

We can cause our own heartache. But we can also prevent it. You don't have to wake up in some strange bed, staring at the ceiling, feeling like crap. Just think—first. Know that the most important person you have to be true to, and the only person you have to answer to, is yourself.

CHAPTER
10

■ ■ ■

GIVE ME BODY!

"Dana, are you wearing a bra?" Miss Tamara asked me. Her question was so direct that I froze in my tracks. I said "No," but I was thinking something like "Hell, no." A bra? I didn't even own a bra.

"Well, you need one," Miss Tamara said.

I was eleven years old, and I had two very unwelcome visitors coming on like gangbusters. At first, I didn't even notice. I was outside playing kickball in front of our house on Littleton Avenue in Newark, running around like a wild woman with the kids from around my way. Just like always.

As Miss Tamara was walking down the street from work, she must have noticed me bouncing around. That's when she pulled me aside to tell me I needed a training bra.

Miss Tamara was this fly lady who had a lot of style, much like my mother. And she was big on the neighborhood girls carrying themselves like ladies.

When I got into the house, my mother noticed me jiggling, too (it must have been the first time those bad boys decided to make an appearance). The next day we went bra shopping. I got a cute, little, white training bra, but the training wheels were off in no time. Before the year was out, I was barely squeezing my new buddies into a 36C. And I was hearing about it.

"Man, you got some big mocongas!"

"What's up, jugs?"

"What you got in your shirt, watermelons?"

"Damn, you got some big a-- titties!"

It's bad enough going through puberty, but to do it in front of the entire neighborhood is mortifying. It's disheartening that the first signs of womanhood—getting your period for the first time, developing breasts—often make a woman feel embarrassed, self-conscious, confused, and inadequate. I know that Miss Tamara meant well and that she just wanted all us neighborhood girls to be tight, but I would have preferred to discover that I needed a bra on my own. My development—like my sexuality—was something I wanted to keep private. Unfortunately, few women have the opportunity to discover themselves on their own. We wind up being uncomfortable with our bodies, because someone is always pointing out the flaws.

If I wasn't dealing with my "too big" breasts, it was my butt, or rather lack thereof. When we moved to Hyatt Court, some of the kids Winki and I used to play with brought to my attention that my pants were sagging in the back.

"Yo, Dana, you have a white girl's booty!" Shawnetta yelled out in front of everyone as I was leaving the rec center. And I couldn't say anything, because she was telling the truth. I used to envy my brother's nice, round behind. Girls used to love his booty, too. I would think, "It's not fair. I'm the one who needs the booty. What do you need with the booty? Give it up. You're a boy!"

If I could only take some of what I had up top and move it to the back.

People look at me now and think, "Wow, there's a full-sized woman who has it together." Puh-lease! It took me years to get to the point where I love my body. And I do truly love my body. But I had to go through stages. I hated my breasts. I hated my butt. I even hated the way I walked. Some girls, with no effort, can just walk cute and ladylike. Not me. I had this lumbering stride that would kind of end up on my toes when I took a step.

Monie Love, whom I met in England while on tour and who performed on my single "Ladies First," has one of the most feminine walks I've ever seen. She doesn't force it. She doesn't even have to try. She just glides through a room. I used to practice and practice, but I still couldn't fix my walk. I felt even more clumsy trying to walk like somebody else. So I said, "Fughetit! I'm just going to walk." I had to accept myself, walk and all.

I am not the prototypical 36-24-36. Never have been, never will be. And although society tells me I'm too big, what I try to keep in my head are words from Maya Angelou. As she says in her poem "Phenomenal Woman," "It's the arch of my back, / The sun of my smile, / The ride of my breasts, / The grace of my style. / I'm a woman . . ."

Television, the movie industry, and the fashion corps tell us that Kate Moss's skin-and-bones look is beautiful. They make Cindy Crawford and Naomi Campbell, Halle Berry, Michelle Pfeiffer, Sandra Bullock, Julia Roberts, Ally McBeal, the entire cast of *Friends* and *Beverly Hills 90210* the standard of beauty. We look at them, and the message that comes through loud and clear is that we need to be thinner, yet bigger-breasted, that we need to flatten our stomachs, lighten our skin, and fill our lips with collagen. We need shorter/longer hair and less of this and more of that. These women are beautiful, but they shouldn't be anyone's standard.

You are the only standard you need. You shouldn't want to look like anybody but you. God made you. And as my mother always told me, "God don't make junk."

Clothes are designed for women size 8 and under— skinny, undernourished, ghost-looking women. When I open fashion magazines, I never see women who represent me and others like me. I see models who are so thin and undeveloped that some of them look like little boys.

As women go about buying clothes to emulate a designer's latest hip ideas, they go for putting on the whole look, rather than adapting the clothes to their own personal style.

I could never fit into the clothes that brighten glossy magazines. But I also hated those "large-size" stores, with half-sizes and X-sizes and dress sizes that went up to senior-citizen ages. I thought the styles were ugly and made me look like an old lady. So I began looking for my own touch and started wearing clothes that fit my personality.

I used to borrow my brother's jeans. I had my own, but I liked his. It used to piss him off, because he would buy a new pair and I would wear them before he did. In no time, the jeans would be worn out to fit my shape, not his. He'd end up giving them to me. My plan all along.

I wore guys' jeans because they came in larger sizes and were more comfortable. I was more concerned about being comfortable than sporting the fashion industry's up-to-the-second dictation of what I should look like. I knew that was a no-win situation. Ironically, it was the need to be comfortable that led to my original image as Queen Latifah.

After I signed with Tommy Boy in 1988, they gave me a few dollars to go out and get an outfit for my promotional pictures. I didn't have a manager at the time, so I was on my own to figure out my image. I knew I wanted to look different from every other rapper—all of whom were rocking the Adidas sweat suits, shell tops, and the big, dookey, gold rope chains. I wasn't down with the gold. I wasn't down with the materialism. I couldn't really afford it, so why front? It didn't make sense to me to rap about and sport all that stuff when I couldn't keep up with the image.

I thought about who I was. Queen Latifah. Delicate, sensitive, kind. A queen like the women of Africa. I didn't need anyone defining an image for me. I already had one. Now it was time to color it in.

I went to an African fabric store on Halsey Street in downtown Newark and found a print top. Most of the outfits were dresses for women and suits for guys. They didn't have anything that suited me. So I created an outfit. I asked the woman who ran the store if she could make me a pair of pants to match the top that I picked out.

For the photo shoot, I was posed, crouching in this funky outfit, with a matching, queenlike hat and no shoes. I couldn't find any shoes that matched what I had on, so I just went without. People went crazy when they saw me.

There was definitely no rapper like this, especially no female rapper—all of whom were either wearing tight clothes and spandex or dressing like the guys in sweat suits or oversized jeans off their butt and T-shirts.

I was breaking the mold.

My gear was all me. It wasn't an act. It was comfortable, flattering, my own style. Everyone else was wearing their sex, but I was wearing my heart. I wanted to be about more than a designer label. I wanted to deliver a message. And people just picked up on it. When I went on my first tour, I wore the same outfit (saved a lot of money), with no shoes, and the crowds went crazy. The Jungle Brothers, who were on tour with me, dubbed me the Mama Zulu.

When you define yourself based on what you like, who you are—and the body and mind that God gave you— eventually people catch up. You don't have to change to fit anybody's preconceived notions. But it's hard to do that when the image that assaults us is a lie. More than 80 percent of people in this country are overweight. That's a reality. But 99.9 percent of what we see and what we want is that supermodel/movie-star body that gets the gorgeous clothes, the stylin' jewelry, and that wins the man. So the majority are trying to fit their square peg into a round hole that wasn't created for them.

Find that square hole and fit in where you fit in.

I'm not eating half a grapefruit a day in order to have my body conform to the mythical "standard." Some women starve themselves to fit into this mold. Jasmine

Guy, the actress who played Whitley on *A Different World* and who starred in the Bob Fosse show *Chicago*, used to talk about the crazy things she'd do to stay thin. She said that in her dancing days, she would put a big apple in her bag and be like, "Ooooh, this will last me for two days!" She wasn't joking. Fuck that! I'd like a meal!

It's a shame that women feel they have to constantly diet and exercise obsessively. They are using good energy to conform to that mythical standard. Think of all the time and money they could be using for a creative pursuit.

I'm about being healthy. And, according to my doctor, I can be healthy at two hundred pounds. And you know when you're healthy. You don't have to go on some crash diet, drink Slim Fast every day, and go crazy to lose weight. I'm not for that. I'm about feeling good at whatever size I am. I know cheese is bad for me. I know a whole bunch of fat and fried foods are bad. I know veggies are good and fruits are good. That's just common sense. Do I not eat cheese, fat, and fried food? Of course I do. But I do it in moderation, because I know the consequences.

You don't have to have a personal trainer and work out every day to look and feel good. When I was growing up, jogging, and then aerobics, became really big. I would see all these aerobics shows on television with these perfectly built women and think, "Give me a break!" There's nothing more annoying than seeing some in-shape person working out. You look at these fitness tapes—everybody's already in shape. How about showing someone who's struggling, and we can get into shape together? Let's watch the progression, how you get from point A to point B.

For me, playing basketball is the answer. I play, not because I want to achieve some greatness on the court (although I like that, too), but because I get a good workout while having fun. And, at the end of a stint on the court, I feel *good*. The challenge, of course, is trying to find the time to play. But recently, I've made it a priority. That's my "me" time. I have decided that staying healthy is going to be a simple pursuit. I've found something that I like to do, and I stay active doing it.

My basketball could be someone else's running around and playing with their kids. You don't have to join a gym and try to look like Miss Bodybuilder America. Play tennis. Walk to the park, and then walk around the park. Just do the things you enjoy and stay active. Watch what you eat and be healthy. But don't try to fit into an image. Do it because *you* want to.

Being firm in body means focussing my mind on being healthy, not skinny. It means figuring out what makes me *feel* good and then making the time to do that.

Very few women I know are completely satisfied with the way they look. For a long time, neither was I. It took me a while to get to the point where I was comfortable with the curve of my back and the "rolls" on my hips— where I could love my body whether I was 165 pounds and buff or 200 with cellulite. Your body, your looks, are not everything that you are. From Newark to New York to Hollywood, I've seen women put so much energy into their looks that I can't find the personality behind all the primping, dieting, and worrying they do about their exterior. Sometimes all I find is vanity. What is behind that?

Men.

There's a point where a woman gets beyond wanting to look good for herself. And that's when she's giving up the power, when she is so focused on looking good for a man that she loses sight of number one. You know the type—she starts getting ready for a night out at three in the afternoon. She's giving herself over to her looks, and in the back of her mind she is wondering, with every stroke of makeup, "Will he like this?" She's becoming dependent on her looks, as if that's all she has to carry her through her days and nights. Women will use their looks to game men. But what happens when that man leaves, or worse, if he never shows up? She may be left with a gorgeous shell, but she hasn't filled up herself inside. She's left feeling empty—and, I'll bet, ugly.

I won't lie. We all want someone to find us attractive. It's part of the circle of life. It's biology. Birds preen to attract the opposite sex. And no one is going to be drawn to a person who is letting herself go, because that represents unhappiness and a lack of self-respect, sure deterrents to any potential suitors. The trick is finding someone who will love you for who you are—whether it's gussied up, glowing from a hot workout, or for your high hair and puffy eyes first thing in the morning. For me, that someone was a guy named Mondo. He loved my big breasts, my flat butt, and my thick waist so much that I would be fool not to love them, too. After years of wanting a different body, I finally felt good about myself.

Sometimes it simply takes a special someone to awaken that good feeling that rests deep within all of us.

Mondo was the man who taught me that beauty is not about a media standard but rather about personal taste. It *is* in the eye of the beholder. He was the first man who really loved me and, as a result, made me feel so good about my "flaws" that I never viewed them as flaws again.

I met Mondo when I was fourteen. We had just moved to Halsted Street in East Orange. He was one of the finest guys in the neighborhood. He played football and was well built, too. Mondo was sixteen but a senior in high school. He was very smart, articulate, and well mannered, and I liked that even more than his good looks. We used to go for long walks through Elmwood Park. It was cool to have a guy I could really talk to without strings and pressure to have sex. It was wonderful puppy love.

Then Mondo went away to college, and we lost touch for a while. But when he got out of school, we started hanging out again and were friends for years before it blossomed into something more. I was Queen Latifah then, rising on the barometer of fame, and it was comforting to be around someone who knew my core. He knew me when.

One night, we were hanging out at my house, watching movies and waiting for some friends to come over and make dinner. I had just come back from a long tour, and I was wiped and exhausted by the thought of having to be in the studio early the next morning. "I'm going to do something nice for you," Mondo said. Then he walked over to where I was, sitting on the floor, leaning against the couch, and he gently guided my body so that I was lying on the floor. And he gave me a massage.

It was the first and best massage I've ever had—and to this day massages are one of my weaknesses. He didn't spare any part of my body. What was wild was that it wasn't really sexual at all; it was very loving. He made me feel like the most beautiful woman in the world, like every part of my body was the best thing he had ever touched.

A few weeks later, I wanted to repay the favor. I had discovered that extra-virgin olive oil made a nice massage oil and took my little concoction over to his place. I had his rubdown all planned out. But as I was getting the bed ready, laying the towels down, putting on the soft music, lighting the incense, he grabbed the oil and told me to lie down.

I was no virgin at this point in my life. I was twenty-one, an adult, but I felt that for the first time I allowed someone to explore my body. Mondo and I had had sex before, but never before had I felt like something more than an object of pleasure for a man. I didn't feel like my breasts and vagina were there just for a man's taking. I realized my entire body could be gratified, adored, nurtured, and loved. He made me feel like all my parts fit together to make a perfect body. I definitely wasn't in the best shape. I wasn't at my thinnest, but Mondo let me know—verbally and physically—that I was perfect. It was like an exclamation point on a statement.

I was never self-conscious about my body again. Nobody could tell me my breasts were too big or my butt was too flat. I wasn't hearing it. I started really loving and appreciating my body. I started sleeping in the nude and walking around my house without clothes on—even when friends were over. They started calling me Naked Girl. I didn't care.

For the first time I was free from all that what-I-should-look-like shit and started loving what I did look like. It was a trip. It took a man to make me feel good about my body. And I think that's okay, because he was lovin' me for what it was, not what I struggled to get it to be.

So much of how we view ourselves physically and sometimes intellectually is based on how other people look at us. Some women do come to love their body through the sensitive touch of a sensitive man. That's not a bad thing, as long as you don't give that man all the power and all the credit and don't stake your entire existence, your self-esteem, on whether he finds you attractive.

Most women, though, allow opinions to make us or break us. If a guy tells you you're beautiful, you believe him. If he says you're ugly, you believe him. Women need to stand strong and set the tone for themselves. Instead, we fall right into that mental trap and end up trying to please guys who are not worthy of our energy. The only real constant should be how you feel about yourself. If you feel good about yourself, there will be a man out there who will see you and feel good about you, too.

I took what Mondo gave me and ran with it. I built on my experience with him. I realized that he alone didn't give me the confidence in my body. He merely cracked that door for me so I could go in and get it for myself, grab it, and keep it growing.

Yes, I love me now, and I am not shy or self-conscious about my body. Part of it was somebody showing me that my body was beautiful, but a bigger part was me allowing that to happen.

When Mondo took that massage oil from me, I could have said no. I could've fallen right back into being self-conscious about my appearance and completely unaware of the pleasure my body could bring me. That's what I was so used to doing—giving pleasure and not expecting much in return. But something clicked with Mondo because he was looking at me differently. I knew right then that I deserved to be treated well, to be treated like a queen. My body was not just someone's sex tool. It was not just an object. It was beautiful and there to be truly admired and loved, especially by its owner, me.

CHAPTER

11

■ ■ ■

MY KING

My father was the first king in my life, and I compared every guy I went out with to my dad. Would this guy be a protector? Would he have my back no matter what, like my dad did? Was he strong? On the flip side, I wondered, 'Did he have vices that controlled his life? Would he cheat on me? Would he betray me?' My father was the strongest, bravest man I had known, but he had also disappointed me more than anyone.

This combination of hope and worry left me confused. I always wanted a man like my father, who could protect me and make me feel safe. Yet I never wanted a man like my father, who could allow his problems and baggage to get in the way of taking care of business with his family.

It's only natural to use the men in your life—your father, brother, best boyfriend from sixth grade—as models of the man you want to be with. But what's not right is to judge every man you come in contact with based on the faults and weaknesses, strengths, and good points of another human being.

Each man is an individual.

I don't subscribe to the theory, "All men are dogs." I give every man in my life the benefit of the doubt. They come into the situation with a free pass, a complete pie. If they choose to eat away at that pie by lying and cheating and doing stupid things, that's on them. Once they eat half, I take my half and I'm gone. I don't wait around for them to eat my half, too.

I almost had a whole pie with Mondo. It was one of the best relationships I've ever known. He wasn't clingy, and he didn't try to control me. He let me be myself, and I loved that about him. But when he left for Rutgers University, we let each other go. And when he came home in the summers, we would bond again and fall right back to where we left off. To this day, we are the best of friends. We are each other's trump card. Like in *My Best Friend's Wedding,* if we don't find anyone else, we will marry each other. It's a fun-loving, comforting thought.

■ ■ ■

The other man who has given me faith in men is Ferric Collons, who used to play defensive end for the Raiders. We met in a Los Angeles club. As I was on my way out, he caught me on the stairs, gently took my hand, and said, "Would you like to go to a football game on Sunday?" This could have been just a line he ran on all the chicks, but I didn't care. I love football. I *wanted* to see a game. It turned out to be a terrific afternoon and the beginning of a wonderful relationship that is now a friendship.

The thing I loved about being with Ferric was that he was not intimidated by me. Too many men can't get past my career, money, fame, because of the independence it affords me. But Ferric had his own career, his own money, and his own fame. Although he respected my autonomy, he didn't translate that into "Dana's untouchable." He knew just the right balance—when to leave me be and when to take the lead.

One fall weekend, when we were in L.A., I told him that I wanted to invest in some art. So we trucked down to Fox Hills Mall, where I fell in love with some paintings by Charles Bibbs. I didn't know the first thing about collecting, but he did, and he offered to negotiate with the dealer. I didn't have to do a thing. I just stood there and watched him get me a great price. It was a small thing, but I felt taken care of.

That was the beginning of a handsome pattern. In the

past six years, I had become the one who did all of the talking, all of the taking care of so many people, whether it was my posse or my mom, and it was like a decadent pleasure just to give myself over to someone. For once, I wasn't the one making the plans, trying to get a group into a club, organizing a trip to the beach. Ferric would just take over a situation. He wouldn't step on my toes. It was the kind of takeover where you didn't mind. It was gentlemanly.

Doors were being opened, manners were being minded.

I know that what enabled me to give myself over to Ferric was that we had mutual interests. We shared a passion for sports and trucks. (He had a big Bronco, jacked up on these high-ass shocks, with an ill sound system. I loved riding with him.) We went to the car show together. That was one advantage of growing up with my brother and dad—I developed a taste for things most men enjoy. And that makes my relationships more complete. They don't have to stop doing the things they love, because they can do them with me; I hold my own in the realm of many interests. I know how to be a woman, of course, and how to be feminine. But cars and sports (and even guns) are stuff that I am genuinely into; I don't have to fake just to be down with a brother. I didn't ask Ferric or other men to give up their interests to spend time with me.

And I didn't give up mine.

Unfortunately, Ferric and I grew apart because our careers took over. He was traded to the Patriots, and I was doing more movies and television. Our schedules clashed. Every now and then, though, he will pick up the phone and ask, "What are you doing this weekend, woman? I'm coming in to see you." And he will come. Being with him is like wearing an old pair of jeans. The comfort level is high, the attitude is relaxed.

Too many women look for what's in a man's pocket, not what's in his heart. All it takes to get over that is meeting a man with a bunch of green (and I've met plenty) and seeing how he descends into a frivolous character who blows it on stupid things. Or, once he's comfortable, his ambition dwindles because he's too busy being content with what he's already accomplished. Or he takes too much for granted. Or he's just an asshole.

I know that tomorrow's not promised and that these gifts that God has given me can be taken away. I look for a person with a similar attitude. If I had a guy who was determined and had his head on straight and had a reality about it, I would stick by him, even if he caught a bump or an obstacle, because I know that man would keep going, keep pushing.

I want my man to be independent, but I also want a man who needs a partner. Most guys I've dated haven't had as much money as I have. But I don't care. I'm interested in whether they are going in the right direction. Who are they as people? And how do they treat me?

Juan knew how to treat me. We met at Borough of Manhattan Community College, in the cafeteria. Every afternoon a group of students would sit in the lunchroom and play spades. I noticed him immediately because he was so damned cute. He was about six-two, with dark, fine, wavy hair. He had a beautiful mouth that kind of sat open when he wasn't talking. He had high cheekbones, sort of like Sylvester Stallone, and these big, dark eyes that made him look like an innocent kid. And he had bo-dy. He was a baseball player, long and lean.

We would say "Hi!" when we saw each other in the cafeteria, but we really didn't start kicking until we hooked up at a club about a year later. I was in the Power House, a club on Twenty-sixth Street in Manhattan, just chilling. Kid Capri was spinning. And this fine guy comes up to me and says, "I know you from BMCC!" It was Juan. We talked all night and danced (he was a good dancer). I was trying to blow up as Queen Latifah, and he had dreams of playing professional baseball. We exchanged numbers and started going out. It was that simple.

I thought he was the one. He could roll with my moods. I laid open all the hidden things in my life. And I dug him for his quirks. Everything about him seemed perfect. Even after playing nine innings of baseball, he smelled sexy. Some guys' funk is so rambunctious you have to run from the room. Not Juan.

But of course, no one is perfect, and you have to be prepared for that from the door. But I'm not looking for perfection. I'm looking for somebody who wants to be a team with me. I want to grow with somebody so that we can spend the rest of our lives together and not wake up in thirty years bored because we are the same people we were in 1999.

As I started becoming successful, Juan seemed to go in the opposite direction. When I met him in college he was a communications major, studying video editing. But he never finished school. He tried out for the Detroit Tigers baseball team and made their Triple-A club. Then he hurt his shoulder, and his career was over. He had to be frustrated, but he never talked about it, and he never did anything to change his situation. Where was his plan B? Soon the man I knew, with verve and ambition, had hit a few bumps and was lying by the road. He was waiting for help, not even trying to get himself up to get it together. I worried about what would happen when we hit bumps. Would he bring me down with him?

Juan and I saw each other, off and on, for a while. I was willing to wait for him to get his act together. When I moved out to California, I wanted him to come with me. But he had a book of excuses about why he couldn't. "I have to work." "My mother needs me." I responded, "If you love me like you say you do and I'm feeling you that, then what's keeping you from being out here?"

Soon I was tired of the sound of my own voice. Those

excuses weren't making it anymore. That's all bullshit. If a man wants to be with you, nothing will stop him. If I want something, nothing will stop me. You can't speak the game through your mouth and have your actions not back it up. You can't tell me this relationship is something you really want and then not make it happen.

You cannot listen to what a man is telling you; you must watch what he does. Apparently Juan didn't have enough faith in our relationship to talk to me honestly about what was going on with him. Instead he ran. I knew something was up. But I chose to ignore my instincts.

Big mistake.

Juan finally came out to see me in L.A. after about a year and a half of not seeing each other. He said he could only take a couple of days, so we had a long weekend together. We went to the Mondrian Sky Bar, one of my favorite restaurants. We went to the House of Blues, where they were having an after-party for the premiere of *Soul Food*. We made love. It was like old times; it was wonderful.

About a day after he left, I got a phone call from a woman I didn't know.

She said she was Juan's girlfriend. She said she knew about me and told him, "If you're going to cheat on me, it had better only be with Queen Latifah because can't no other woman hold a candle to me." I was flattered and amused. And then hurt. So she was the "roommate" he had told me about. Juan had been deceptive. We had been apart so much that I hadn't thought he was living as a monk, but I resented that he misrepresented the facts. What else was he holding back?

Ironically, I had written a rap on *Black Reign* about Juan. Although the details of the situation turned out a little differently, I must have had some sort of premonition and I chose to ignore it:

> A brother pushed up on me at the movies one weekend
> We was on a quest and I was who he was seekin'.
> And although I am black and he was a Puerto Rican
> Ain't make no dif to me so we continued to speak
> And we hit it right off and everything was on a roll
> Before I knew it I was in love with his soul
> I, poppi, I, was the cry as he made love to me
> I was freed by the way he used to do me.
>
> And then one day while I was washing his clothes,
> A name fell out of his pocket, and her name was Rose.
> A girl's number, hmmm, that struck me kind of funny
> I lost my grip. I had to call up the honey
> (There was a chick on the side)
> Oh, no, it couldn't be
> (There was a chick on the side)
> He's down with OPP?
> I gave him the whole shabang
> To find another woman working my thang.
>
> —"I Can't Understand"

One of the worst enemies to a woman's self-esteem is other women. When I was growing up, it was the girls I hung out with who teased me about my "white girl's booty" and my large breasts. They were the ones who made me self-conscious about not looking so-called normal. They were the ones not the guys, who made me question myself. We girls were competitive and territorial. And that made us disrespectful. But we were girls.

There is nothing more disrespectful than for a *woman* to knowingly sleep with another's man. I don't care how unhappy that brother says he is or whatever "problems" he says he's going through in the relationship, you lower yourself and disrespect his woman by sleeping with him. If a man tells you, "Yo, I have a girl," and you say that's cool and date him anyway, you're disrespecting his woman. Now, if he doesn't tell you or lies to you, that's another story. But there are too many women out there willing to do whatever. And what comes around goes around. It will happen to you.

More than anything, I see number one women out there dating married men. By number one women I mean women who should be a man's wife, not a man's mistress. And, as a result, they trade in their number one status for a role as an extra, a member of the supporting cast. Because so many women are willing to allow a man to have his cake and eat it, too, it makes it hard on the rest of us self-respecting, taking-no-crap sisters. These women who are willing to play second fiddle make it acceptable for a man to be a player.

If everybody would stop sleeping with everybody else's man, if women would stop giving up their bodies so quick, it might bring us back to the times when a man would earn a woman's affection. I wish those days would come back. Women felt special, and men stepped up to the plate and showed their dignity.

We live in permissive times, but that doesn't mean we have to be easy. You think that if you sex him out better than he's ever had it in his life, he's going to stay? If you gave it up to him so quickly, what makes you think he's going to be able to trust you? He may think, if you gave it to him so quick, why wouldn't you do the same for the next guy? See, you're not making that man feel special, either. Play a little hard to get. Wait. Slow down. Believe me, he'll respect you for it in the end. And there will be rewards.

In retrospect, I realize that Juan was just too insecure to be real. Ultimately, he moved to Virginia and started hustling drugs, which, to me, seemed so out of character. He started to talk more like a "street n---a." He traded in his Budweiser for Hennessey and started smoking cigarettes. He was running around being someone that he wasn't, when all I ever wanted was the nice, mild-mannered, clean-cut guy with the beautiful smile and mad love for hard-core hip-hop that I knew. He was trying to live up to an image that wasn't him. That's not who I met, and that's not who I fell in love with. He felt intimidated being with me, and he wasn't man enough to say it. I didn't care whether he made a lot of money. I knew he wasn't in a position to take care of me financially. All I wanted was the man who understood Dana from day one.

One of the major problems women have in relationships is thinking, "If I could just meet the right man, all my problems would be over." Hell, no. What's that? If you're broken, no man is going to fix you. No one can do anything for someone who isn't okay with herself. Everything comes back to you. If you're living right and if you're right, you *will* find the man you're meant to be with. How do you expect to meet Mr. Right when you're Ms. Wrong? How much sense does that make? And, if the guy you're tripping over is so great, does he deserve to have half a woman or a woman who isn't correct? You have to work on you first, develop yourself, and be confident and comfortable before Mr. Right can even have a chance to be in your life. You have to wonder about a man who is drawn to a troubled woman. What's he looking for? A man like that is likely to make it worse. The person you're meant to be with will reveal himself in time. Be patient, ladies. Fix yourself, get complete, get whole. Then, like magic, you will attract a whole, complete man who will do right by you.

There are good guys out there. But everybody's human, and you have to look at it that way. There's no perfection in women and no perfection in men. There are people who are compatible and people who love one another and learn how to work with one another and fit with one another. You need a balance. I click with a lot of opposites, in both relationships and friendships. I love people with whom I have something in common, but I am also turned on by someone whose strength is my weakness, whose passion is something I've never heard of. Those are the people who give me new perspective. We fill in the slots for each other.

When I looked into the future, I could see me and Juan getting married. I saw us having kids, beautiful kids. I saw us building a life together. But he couldn't see beyond his own shortcomings. So he missed out. And I moved on. I still miss him. We haven't talked since around the time I found out about the other girlfriend. Being a girl, I have dialed his number once just to see who would answer. (Haven't we all done that?) Her voice was on the answering machine: "I'm not in at the moment . . ." I. What happened to we? I wondered if she put him out. But, aside from the occasional memories and flashbacks, I'm pushing forward. You have to. You have to move on. There's a whole big world out there.

I'm ready to explore the possibilities.

I think a lot about getting married and having kids. I think about having kids more than getting married, though. I want to be married first and then have my children. I ain't going to judge anyone who doesn't get married, but that's not what I want to happen for me. I would love to know who Mr. Right will be, who will be the father of my children, and who will plan birthday parties and college funds and change diapers with me.

I get frustrated at times. Like a lot of women, I am anxious about these issues. And as I get older, I'm not relaxing any. I don't want to be too old having and raising kids. But, at the same time, I know what's most important: finding the right person and getting to know him so well that I would trust him to raise our kids. What if something happens to me and my husband has to take over? Is he the man who can do that? He must be.

From time to time, I consider adopting. Rosie O'Donnell is a great example of a woman who is raising a family alone and balancing a great career. I look at her and know that it can be done. I am comforted and inspired. But at the same time, there's still that old-fashioned thing. I don't want to do it alone. I know that inside of me is a woman who is ready for a commitment and ready to make a sacrifice to have a solid relationship.

But, if he doesn't exist, if I don't get my king, I also know I can be by myself. A man does not make you a queen. And a man cannot complete you. So I focus on growing spiritually, strengthening my relationship with

God—the first and true King in my life—and being the best person I can be. If I'm happy with me first, everything else is gravy.

So, for now, because it's what I want, I pray on finding the man to share my life with. I know he will be revealed in time.

I keep the faith.

12

■ ■ ■

EVERY WOMAN HAS

A CALL

In the Bible, the apostle Paul talks about *learning* contentment.

> ...I have learned, in whatsoever state I am, therewith to be content. I know both how to be abased, and I know how to abound: every where and in all things I am instructed both to be full and to be hungry, both to abound and to suffer need. I can do all things through Christ which strengtheneth me.
>
> —Philippians 4:11–13

We live in a society that tells—promises—us that material things breed contentment. If we possess and own, if we satisfy our desires, we will be happy. And if we don't, we'll be miserable. If you don't drive the right kind of car, you are pitiful. If you don't sport the latest Air Jordans, the phattest gear, you're considered a Herb. If you don't have a lot of money, you're weak. And if you don't have a man, you're not a complete woman. The media tells us this. Sometimes our friends suggest as much, and often our parents may even make us feel inadequate. And we tell ourselves these same lies. We run after *things* as if our whole being depended on it.

I know a lot of people who think that this world owes them something. It's an easy attitude to come by. I am guilty of having felt that I deserve my real friends after giving myself to people who took advantage of me. That I warrant success and fame and all of my dreams because I've worked my ass off and made a lot of money for a lot of people. I have even felt that I am due some heavy compensation for all the pain that came from losing those close to me and losing myself. "Shouldn't I get true love? Don't I deserve a break?" I have caught myself thinking.

Life doesn't owe me—or anyone—a thing.

Everything that you are, everything that you can be, starts inside of you and it starts with God. Nothing can take the place of a great friendship, a true love, or a big brother. There isn't a deal, a contract, a car, a bank account, or a promise that can mend a broken heart or make you believe in yourself.

The one thing that keeps me grounded is knowing that God created me in Her image. He made me to be just like Her. My capabilities and my possibilites are endless. I have the potential to create, to heal, to comfort, to love, to be the best me I can possibly be. Once you realize what you can do and who you are, you can relax in the confidence of being you. In *Conversations with God*, Neale Donald Walsch says that life is not like school, where you have to learn, but it is a process of experiences, where you ultimately remember who you are. You are given what you need for life at birth, and you spend this life remembering what was placed in you, remembering who you are. But what reminds you?

You.

You can't find out who you are and what you're made of if you're too afraid to look hard at yourself. I would be lost if I hadn't stared myself down. I looked at myself through the eyes of my mother and God. And at times I didn't like what I saw. But I was the only one with the power to change it. I had to wake myself up, slap myself in the face, and realize who I was—and who I wasn't. And be me.

And now I just keep reaching for that mark. Every day I have to remind myself of my core.

As Queen Latifah, I have had so many people slap

images and labels on me. People have expectations of who they think I am or who they think I should be. But I am not just the outer covering that people see. I don't have to wear a sign that says I AM QUEEN LATIFAH for people to treat me with respect. I command it. And I don't need Queen Latifah to be a queen. All I need is to be myself.

To get to the point of being myself, though, I had to go through a whole bunch of years of being something *other* than myself. I went through the tomboy stage. The not-feeling-good-about-my-body stage. The awkward-sex stage. The giving-up-my-sex-for-money stage. The running-wild stage. The doing-drugs stage. The wanting-to-die stage. And I realized they were extremely valuable stages to go through. They were part of life's process.

As I continue to grow in my queenliness, I've learned that there is no greater quality than contentment. It is the mother of peace. But the apostle Paul isn't talking about *getting* contentment, he's talking about *growing into* it. He's saying that it comes from what we have *within* us, not *around* us. I can be content in every situation, as the apostle Paul says, because I know that each experience, each hardship, each joyous occasion, is simply preparing me for the next level, the next layer of me. I ride it out and see where it takes me.

The power to be who I wanted to be was—and is— with me the whole time. We all have the power to be the person we set our sights on being. We have the power to change our lives so that we are at peace. It is just a matter of using that power in the right way. *Power.* The word goes with being a queen. The key is not to rule others but to reign over yourself. As free people, we have the power to constantly reevaluate and remake ourselves. We are always evolving.

But don't confuse having the power with controlling every situation in your life. You can only control the way you respond to situations; you can't always control events. Do you fly off the handle, throw tantrums, and bug out every time something inconvenient or bad happens? Or do you ride it out, knowing that "this too shall pass"? Do you view every situation as a problem? Do you bitch and complain all the time? Or do you make the best of everything? Contentment, peace, starts within. Whom do you see when you look at yourself? A person who is always worried, nervous, and anxious? Or a person who is made in the image of God?

There is plenty in life that our power can't touch. When Winki died, it was the most painful, tragic thing ever to come into my life. For the longest time, I threw energy into wanting to bring Winki back. I wanted my mom to heal. I wanted peace for my father. I couldn't stop the pain. I was self-destructive. My hand was a fist, and I could not recover from the grief.

But the time of my brother's death was also a period of intense evolution for me. That day, sitting in church, a year after Winki's death, I achieved a milestone. I had carried on—lived, loved, and made an award-winning album—through—and because of—unimaginable pain.

I take nothing for granted anymore. I am grateful for every blessing in my life.

> You think you're living right
> But we know it's nonsense
> In case you forgot just
> Check your conscience
> At showtime I blow lines
> You don't get yours, I get mine
> You show signs you're behind
> The Queen Latifah divine
> Rule no. 1: Don't step across
> The line that I drew
> Rule No. 2: Don't take credit for something
> You didn't do
> No. 3: Check your heart
> Every man has a call
> It's time for me to go
> But I'll be back, y'all
> —"Latifah's Law," *All Hail the Queen*

Find power. Find the queen who lives inside of you, embrace her, nourish her, praise her, hold her accountable, and love her.

Become her.